Group Music Activities for Adults with Intellectual and Developmental Disabilities

of related interest

Activities for Adults with Learning Disabilities
Having Fun, Meeting Needs
Helen Sonnet and Ann Taylor
ISBN 978 1 84310 975 4

Promoting Social Interaction for Individuals
with Communicative Impairments
Making Contact
Edited by M. Suzanne Zeedyk
ISBN 978 1 84310 539 8

Using Intensive Interaction with a Person with a Social
or Communicative Impairment
Graham Firth and Mark Barber
ISBN 978 1 84905 109 5

Pied Piper
Musical Activities to Develop Basic Skills
John Bean and Amelia Oldfield
ISBN 978 1 85302 994 3

Let's All Listen
Songs for Group Work in Settings that Include Students
with Learning Difficulties and Autism
Pat Lloyd
Foreword by Adam Ockelford
ISBN 978 1 84310 583 1

Group Music Activities for Adults with Intellectual and Developmental Disabilities

Maria Ramey

Jessica Kingsley *Publishers*
London and Philadelphia

First published in 2011
by Jessica Kingsley Publishers
116 Pentonville Road
London N1 9JB, UK
and
400 Market Street, Suite 400
Philadelphia, PA 19106, USA

www.jkp.com

Library of Congress Cataloging in Publication Data
Ramey, Maria.
  Group music activities for adults with intellectual and developmental
disabilities / Maria Ramey.
     p. cm.
  Includes bibliographical references and index.
  ISBN 978-1-84905-857-5 (alk. paper)
  1. Music therapy. 2. Music for the developmentally disabled. 3. Music for
people with mental disabilities. I. Title.
  ML3920.R17 2011
  615.8'5154--dc22
                          2010047994

British Library Cataloguing in Publication Data
A CIP catalogue record for this book is available from the British Library

ISBN 978 1 84905 857 5

Printed and bound in Great Britain

Contents

Acknowledgments   9

Preface   11

How to Use This Book   17

Activities   **21**

[The originator of each activity is identified by her initials]

1. Play the Tambourine (KM)   23

2. Smile and Wave (MK)   24

3. I Like to Sing (KS)   25

4. Let's All Play Together (KS)   26

5. Scarf Dance (MK)   27

6. I'm in the Mood (MK)   28

7. The Weekend Song (MR)   29

8. You Are My Sunshine (MR)   30

9. Triangle Teams (MK)   31

10. Shaking to the Music Beat (MR)   32

11. Live Music Relaxation (VO)   33

12. Shake up High (MR)   34

13. Visual Lyric Analysis (MR)   35

14. Cluster Drumming (MK)   36

15. Pick a Card: Instruments (MR)   37

16. Frame Drum Imagination (MK)   38

17. Heartbeat (MR)   39

18. Over the Rainbow (MR)   40

19. I Love… (SK)   41

20. Old MacDonald Had a Band (MK)   42

21. Clap Your Hands, One Two Three (MK)   43

22. I Feel Good (CF)   44

23. Matching Loud and Soft (MK)   45

24. Just for Fun (MR)   46

25. Paint the Air (MR)   47

26. Howl at the Moon (KS)   48

27. Twelve Days (MK)   49

28. Random Duet (MR)   50

29. Emotion Connection (VO)   51

30. Stretchy Band Hokey Pokey (MK)   52

31. Concerto Soloist (MR)   53

32. Conducting (MK)   54

33. Guess the Hidden Instrument (MK)   55

34. How Many Beats? (LF)   56

35. Walkin' Down the Street (LF)   57

36. Walk Like the Music (KS)   58

37. Visual CDs (KS)   59

38. Pick a Card: Feelings (MR)   60

39. Jump and Jive (SK)   61

40. Mirroring (SK)   62

41. Twist (MR)   63

42. Follow My Beat (MR)   64

43. My Favorite Things (MR)   65

44. Cha, Cha, Cha (KM)   66

45. Signs of the Seasons (MK)   67

46. Manic Monday (LF)   68

47. News from Home (VO/MR)   69

48. Traveling Places (MK)   70

49. Colors Everywhere (MR)   71

50. Nature Box (MR)   72

51. This Is Me (MR)   73

52. Wave the Scarves (KM)   74

53. Shake a Question (MR)   75

54. Guess That Sound (MR)   76

55. Clap Your Hands to the Music (KM)   77

56. Move to the Music (KM)   78

57. Dance Conducting (MR)   79

58. Marching In (MR)   80

59. Song Bingo (KM)   81

60. Musical Ball (SK)   82

61. Musical Feelings (MR)   83

62. Party Animal (MR)   84

63. Celebration Song (MR)   85

64. Drum Q&A (MK)   86

65. Rhythm Sticks Alphabet (MK)   87

66. Your Story Through a Song (VO)   88

67. Five Letter Favorites (MK)   89

68. Boom Boom (LF)   90

69. I Won't Back Down (LF)   91

70. Leadership: African Drumming (LF)   92

71. Marching Band (LF)   93

72. Eye Choose You (MR)   94

73. What I Like About You (MR)   95

74. I Can See Clearly Now (LF)   96

75. Xylophone Conversation (MR)   97

76. Boomwhacker Beat (MR)   98

77. The Music Comes Over (MR)   99

78. You Are (KM)   100

79. Collective Mandala (MR)   101

80. Turn, Turn, Turn (LF)   102

81. Simple Songwriting (KS)   104

82. Musical Shapes (MR)   105

83. Animal Adventure (MR)   106

84. Do-Re-Mi Chimes (MR)   108

85. Roll Your Fists Around (KM)   109

86. Rhythm Shakers (MR)   110

87. Rhythmic Hot Potato (KS)   111

88. Shake, Rattle and Roll (MR)   112

89. Film Scoring (KS)   113

90. Musical Charades (MS)   114

91. Collaborative Drawing (MR)   115

92. Color to the Instruments (KM)   117

93. Musical Board Game (KM)   119

94. Guitar Strum (KS)   121

95. Rhythm Pies (KS)   122

96. Music Listening Game (MK)   123

97. Index Card Songwriting (SK)   124

98. Chordal Songwriting (VO)   125

99. Xylophone Ensemble (KS)   126

100. Creative Sing-a-longs (MR)   127

Appendix A: Sheet Music for Original Songs   129

Appendix B: List of Books Illustrating Well-Known Songs   145

Appendix C: List of Songs Referred to in Activities   147

Appendix D: Supply Resources   149

Appendix E: Contributors   151

Appendix F: Activities Listed by Goal Area   153

Appendix G: CD Track Listing   169

References   171

Acknowledgments

I would like to thank:

My husband Ryan and our three children, Autumn, Tristan and Zander, for always believing in me and for being willing to fend for yourselves during the time needed to finish this book. I am blessed to have such a wonderful family.

My graduating music-therapy class at California State University, Northridge. It is my sincere belief that the sharing of ideas sparks the inspiration of new ideas, and I will be forever grateful for the warm camaraderie in which we were able to share our ideas.

Professor Ron Borczon, whose enthusiasm for music therapy is contagious and inspiring, and whose teaching sets students on a clear pathway toward success. Thank you for always expecting the best.

Minako Kamimura, the best internship supervisor one could ask for and now a truly wonderful colleague. Thank you so much for your support and friendship.

My other contributors: Lindsay Felchle, Kiho Moriwaki, Kelly Summer, Vera Otsuka and Susie Kwon. Your excitement, support and great ideas are what made this book possible. Thank you from the bottom of my heart.

Hope University staff and students. You are my second family! And you are the inspiration for this book. Thank you.

Preface

While browsing some online bookstores one day for inspiration, I came across several comprehensive collections of fully developed activity ideas for art therapists. I began to wonder whether similar resources existed for music therapists, and more specifically, for therapists working with adults with intellectual and developmental disabilities. What a tremendous resource something like that could be, not only for therapists new to the field but also for those with experience who might need new ideas here and there to refresh creativity and renew excitement for their work. Further searching led me to discover that there are in fact very few activity idea resources currently available for music therapists working with persons with developmental disabilities, and what is available is not age appropriate for adults.

Troubled by what I'd found (or hadn't found), I decided to create my own collection of group music activities for this population organized in a format that is easy to understand and reference. It is my belief that the sharing of ideas and experience is the most important tool we as music therapists have to advance our profession and to maximize the positive impact we have on our clients. As of 2006, in the United States of America alone, there were 4.7 million adults with intellectual and developmental disabilities (Braddock, Hemp and Rizzolo 2008). Music therapists working with this population should be able to find the resources they need to assist them in this profession which profoundly touches so many lives.

The activities in this book recognize the age and interests of our adult clients while remaining accessible within the limits of their disabilities. These limits often include childlike comprehension, social skills and behavior, and we walk a fine line teaching skills in a way that can be understood without treating the client like a child. In addition to creating understandable frustration and resentment in the client, treating them like children puts up a large roadblock in their ability to move forward and reach their goals. As John Meyers (2008) explains, "Treating adults with developmental disabilities like a child just lowers everyone's expectations of them...especially of themselves" (p.21).

The activities presented here have been designed to raise expectations and provide skill-building techniques in ways that will not cause the client to feel as though they are being treated like a child, recognizing, however, that what appeals to and is effective for these clients may seem childishly simple at first glance. We are, after all, addressing areas of cognition and skill that are developmentally delayed compared to the chronological age of the client.

All of the activities included in this book have been used effectively with this population by currently practicing music therapists. These are previously unpublished original ideas from myself and from my contributors; however, it must be noted that some ideas may have been influenced by others, whether we are aware of this influence or not. Also, some ideas, particularly those tied to specific songs, may be conceived by multiple persons who are not in collaboration. In fact, during the collection of ideas for this book, several instances came up where very similar or identical ideas were submitted by more than one contributor, each unaware that their activity had in fact also been thought of by someone else. Such is the nature of this field, with our shared training and desire to provide creative avenues of success for our clients.

In addition to the target population of adults with developmental disabilities, many activities in this book may also be used appropriately and effectively with persons who have memory impairment, cognitive impairment due to traumatic or organic brain damage, children with developmental disabilities and many others whose goal areas are similar. It is my hope that this book will become a valuable resource for music therapists, music-therapy students, activity directors and other persons who are responsible for providing stimulating musical activities for these populations.

Where it all started

The beginning of music therapy with this population has strong ties to a woman named Juliette Alvin, an English music therapist in the 1950s and 1960s who used her cello to interact with people with developmental disabilities, many of whom were living in psychiatric institutions at that time. She found that interacting musically with these patients provided great benefit (Schalkwijk 2000). Alvin went on to teach others what she had learned. Playing music with this population remains an important component of therapists' work with them, drawing them out to interact socially and develop necessary skills to work with others.

Meanwhile, in the early 1960s, Paul Nordoff and Clive Robbins pioneered highly successful improvisational music-therapy programs in the United States at daycare centers and schools, working with children with development disabilities in addition to those physically handicapped or emotionally disturbed. Word of the pair's success spread quickly, and they toured extensively worldwide to educate and train others, particularly flourishing in London, where they established the Nordoff-Robbins Music Therapy Centre in 1974 (now known as the Nordoff Robbins Centre). Nordoff-Robbins music therapy continues to be a strong and successful approach worldwide to working with the intellectually and developmentally disabled population, children and adults alike, using improvisation and tailoring every session to individual clients.

Other angles of approach to music therapy in general and to music therapy with this specific population are also taught and practiced successfully. The various approaches to music therapy are not discussed here; this book is not meant to be a textbook but rather an idea resource for all music therapists, who can modify the activities as dictated by their training, values, individual clients and situations.

Why music?

Music is a highly successful therapy with nearly any population because of its universal connection and creative adaptability. The reasons for its success with the developmentally disabled population include the inherent social nature of music, its strengths as a tool for memory establishment and recall, and the order it creates from chaos. Edith Hillman Boxill, a well-known advocate, practitioner and teacher of music therapy for adults with developmental disabilities, summarized the reasons for the use of music therapy with this population by listing what music can do.

> The rationale for using music therapy as a primary treatment modality for developmentally disabled persons follows. Used as a therapeutic tool, music:
>
> - effects direct contact on a psychobiological basis with people who often are otherwise unreachable;
> - serves to establish, maintain and strengthen the client-therapist relationship in ways that are uniquely attributable to the power of this tool;

- facilitates expression in people who either are nonverbal or have deficits in communication skills;

- provides the opportunity for experiences that open the way for, and motivate, learning in all domains of functioning;

- creates the opportunity for positive, successful and pleasurable social experiences not otherwise available to them;

- develops awareness of self, others and the environment that improves functioning on all levels, enhances well-being and fosters independent living.

(Boxill 1985, p.16)

While persons with severe to profound levels of intellectual or developmental disability will respond quite positively to one-on-one music therapy and often in fact need it most, individuals with moderate or mild developmental disabilities will benefit most from the group setting. The needs of this population center greatly on social skills and awareness, making the group setting ideal for development, particularly when using music and its powerful social attributes.

Creating a successful music-therapy group

Control the environment

Minimize distractions and maximize focus. Ideally, you should hold sessions in a dedicated room that is neither cramped nor overly spacious. Avoid the use of soft chairs that people may fall asleep in, maintain a comfortable room temperature and avoid scheduling soft music groups in a room next to a loud drum circle. Having the clients sit in a circle also helps maximize focus because people can't sleep, carry on private conversations or perseverate on other things as easily as they would otherwise. The circle also helps everyone in the group feel equally included and important, and increases eye contact. If a table is needed for an activity, use one that everyone can sit around together. Also be aware of clients who tend to distract one another if they are seated next to each other, and of clients who do well together.

Know your clients

Medication side effects, co-morbid psychiatric conditions and family issues may cause unexpected behavioral problems or affect a client's response to certain activities. Get to know your clients' charts and make it a point to become informed about important changes in your clients' lives, and you will be better able to provide a successful experience for them.

Expect success

Never underestimate your clients. They will respond to higher expectations with more effort and will achieve higher success. Believe in them and they can believe in themselves. Even when a client has repeatedly failed in a particular task, keep trying and remain positive. Your next try may create just the final push or amount of demonstration they need to make the connection and achieve success. It could even be the turning point that leads to increased success all around. If you are passing a microphone around the group for turn-taking in singing something and there's that one client who never holds onto anything and doesn't seem interested in or able to use the microphone, don't pass her over. Hold the microphone up to her and encourage her to try. She just might take that microphone this time and surprise you with a song of her own.

Make positive reinforcement a full-time habit

Members of this population have spent their entire lives hearing about what they cannot do well. They need recognition for what they can do and will be inspired to keep trying. Giving out positive reinforcement is something you've likely been well trained in, but it's easy to forget or to do infrequently because you feel like you're always saying the same things. Being specific, as in "Great job playing softly" or "Thanks for looking at me when you answered the question!", rather than just saying "Good job", will help you avoid saying the same thing every time. Genuine, personal reinforcement is especially important when working with individuals who are often patronized and dismissed.

Keep directions clear and simple

Cognitive difficulties may prevent many of your clients from grasping instructions with multiple steps, especially if each step is complex. Make your instructions as simple as possible with few words, and demonstrate/practice each step before moving on to the next one. Also keep the pace of the activities client-driven. Stay relaxed, and don't feel you have to move quickly just to get through all of the things you had planned.

Respect your clients

There is a fine line between keeping those directions simple and talking down to your clients. Developmental disabilities and other characteristics of conditions present in your clients (particularly in Down's syndrome) may create a child-like illusion, and it can be easy to address these clients as though they were children. Respect them as adults, give them choices and don't address them with childish nicknames. Respect should be mutual; your modeling of the way to properly treat other adults will be a great example for your clients to follow. Part of respecting your clients involves using age-appropriate activities with them and choosing appropriate songs. You may occasionally use a tune that is typically associated with childhood in order to provide a familiar point for the clients to grasp, but change the words to make it more age appropriate. Activity 20, "Old MacDonald Had a Band," is one example of this technique.

Believe in your ability to improvise

Most of us feel most comfortable when we have things completely planned out ahead of time. If you haven't been trained in improvisation, it may be something you'll deliberately have to work on, but you will find it is well worth the risk and effort. Improvisation may involve deciding in the moment what activity works best with a particular group at that time, creating a new activity based on interests that group members express right then, simply improvising music together or even the spontaneous composition of new music. "The Weekend Song" was composed spontaneously one day, when the group I was working with was hyper and distracted, not quite ready to focus on group activities. I asked a client what he had done over the weekend and instead of answering, he engaged in animated gestures with another client. I began playing chords on my guitar to bring focus back to myself and repeated my question through song, allowing the melody to come naturally. The entire group instantly turned their attention to me and became fully engaged in this spontaneous activity, eagerly awaiting their turn to be asked about their weekend. Clients who didn't usually share many details spoke more specifically about people they had seen and places they had gone. The song is simple and short, but it has become a client favorite. I've since been asked many times to "sing 'The Weekend Song.'"

Be ready for anything

When planning your activities, imagine your particular clients participating in the activity: What might go wrong? Will you be ready for that? Have extra activities ready in the back of your mind, in case what you have planned doesn't work out or the time flies by more quickly than you've anticipated. You should also be prepared to cut activities short or leave something out if your clients spend more time on an activity than anticipated. Mentally preparing for these things in advance is an exercise that will not only help you feel more confident in the long run but will also help you be more flexible in the moment, prepared to improvise at any time during a session—to be ready for anything.

How to Use This Book

The activities in this book are designed to teach appropriate behavior through musically guided repetition, introduce life skills in a format that is supportive and non-threatening, and stimulate an internal awareness and desire to learn and practice these skills. Guided client improvisation is also built into many of these activities as a way to encourage self-awareness and expression.

All activities can and should be modified as needed to fit your group of clients and can also be used as inspirational springboards to creating new activity ideas specific to your clients. The activities in this book are not designed to be used primarily with persons with severe to profound developmental disabilities; however, many of the activities may be adapted to these clients, particularly in a mixed-group setting.

Be prepared to change your instructions and/or expectations for each client in the group. For example, if an activity suggests that each person answers an open question and a particular client is unable to do this, modify the question to have a yes/no answer, ask the rest of the group what they think the client's answer might be, or suggest an answer yourself and watch for clues that the client agrees or disagrees with you. If the activity calls for each client to come up with a certain creative movement or sound and this is too difficult for some clients, watch for some small movement or sound they may spontaneously make and treat this as though it was a deliberate choice (it may well have been!). Be creative and expect success. Your belief in your clients will come across in your body language and voice and will inspire them to reach new heights. Many activities in this book include specific suggestions for activity adaptation in the cases of wheelchair dependence, clients with limited or no verbal skills and those with cognitive difficulties.

The included activities have been arranged in approximate order of difficulty. This assessment of difficulty is subjective, however, and you are encouraged to try activities of all levels. This is especially important when your group is made up of persons with widely varying cognitive, physical and social skills who may respond differently to various challenges. The 100th activity in this book is a collection of various ways to conduct creative sing-a-longs. The power of the sing-a-long to enhance focus, participation and other areas should not be overlooked. This activity suggests ways to take the sing-a-long a step further and keep it both fun and therapeutic.

The term *client* has been used in the opening sections of this book because it is a universal term among music therapists; however, the terms *group members* or *participants* will be used throughout the activity section of this book to refer to the persons in the group who are participating in the activity. This distinction is made to respect the fact that facilitators implementing these activities may prefer and use the term *patient, resident* or a term other than *client*.

Many goal areas and specific objectives may be addressed through group music therapy. The activities in this book are designed to address several goal areas at once, making them effective for groups of clients who may have differing needs. Common goal areas for adults with intellectual and developmental disabilities have been identified and broken down into subcategories for this book and are summarized as follows.

Communication skills

Auditory perception: Recognizing and responding appropriately to sound sources.

Receptive language: Understanding and following directions.

Expressive language: Making needs, thoughts or feelings understood through speech.

Initiating contact and communication: Actively creating an interaction with someone else.

Academic skills

Counting/Math: Math and pre-math skills.

Reading: Reading and comprehension.

Other: Color recognition, geography, art skills and music history.

Cognitive skills

Sequencing: Understanding and implementing steps in a task.

Abstract thinking: Applying unseen concepts and ideas to concrete reality.

Analyzing: Taking concepts apart to delve below the surface and discover how they work.

Reality orientation: Establishing a presence in the here and now, understanding past/present/future and putting memories in order.

Memory: Retaining and recalling facts.

Attention span: Maintaining focus for appropriate lengths of time.

Sensorimotor

Gross motor: Range and controlling movement of large muscle groups such as arms, legs, trunk and neck/head.

Fine motor: Controlling movement of the small muscle groups, such as finger dexterity.

Sensory integration: Combining use of multiple senses to increase awareness and cognitive connections.

Social/emotional skills

Identify/appropriately express emotion: Identifying, analyzing, understanding and properly expressing feelings.

Turn-taking: Exercising patience and following socially appropriate expectations.

Teamwork: Working with other persons to achieve the same goal; demonstrating patience, helpfulness and both leadership and submissive qualities appropriately.

Impulse control: Implementing self-control to maintain socially appropriate behavior.

Self-esteem: Increasing positive self-awareness and acceptance.

Other: Appropriate verbal interaction, eye contact, group support and an understanding of individuality.

Leisure skills

Imagination/creativity: Actively using imagination and developing creative skills and techniques.

Musical skill: Developing musical performance skills.

Music appreciation: Developing awareness of and appreciation for complexities in music.

Relaxation: Pursuing musically guided physical relaxation.

You will find a list of all the activities contained in the book grouped by category and subcategory in Appendix F.

Finally, these activities were developed by and for music therapists; however, many activities may easily be facilitated by care providers who are not trained in music therapy but have training in music performance or education. This use is encouraged only when a music therapist is not available and when the activities would be beneficial to the clients; however, it is important to note that if the activity is not led by a trained music therapist, the session should not be thought of or referred to as *music therapy* but rather as a *music activity* or simply, *music*. Music therapists are professionals who have been extensively trained in the use of music as a psychotherapeutic, skill-building or physically guiding tool, and have been educated in psychiatric illnesses, special education, group dynamics and music facilitation. Take care to avoid creating or bringing issues to light that you are not trained to deal with.

Above all else, have fun and enjoy what your clients have to offer you. They can be quite creative, too.

Activities

1. Play the Tambourine

Goal areas

- Communication skills: *Initiating contact and communication*
- Social/emotional skills: *Turn-taking, Other*

Materials

- Tambourine
- Guitar or piano

Activity

Ask for a volunteer or designate a group member to be the first leader. Give this leader the tambourine and have her walk around the group, holding out the tambourine to each person to play by tapping on it. Sing a well-known song as a group, as the tambourine is being taken around and played. Give everyone a chance to be the leader.

Notes

♪ You may use recorded music instead of live music, if you need to assist the leader in going around the group.

2. Smile and Wave

Goal areas

- Communication skills: *Receptive language*
- Social/emotional skills: *Identify/appropriately express emotion*

Materials

- Guitar or piano
- Music for "Smile and Wave" by Minako Kamimura (See Appendix A)

Activity

Sing the song "Smile and Wave" to each of the group members, encouraging them to smile and wave while singing their answers.

Notes

♪ Instead of "Smile and Wave," try other gestures such as nod, stomp, clap, etc. These may be either designated by you or suggested by each person before you sing the song.

♪ "Smile and Wave" can be used as a hello song to open the session.

3. I Like to Sing

Goal areas

- Communication skills: *Auditory perception*
- Leisure skills: *Musical skill*

Materials

- Guitar or piano (optional)
- Music for the song "I Like to Sing" by Minako Kamimura (See Appendix A)

Activity

Sing the song "I Like to Sing" with the group echoing the leader. Group members may take turns being the leader if they choose.

Notes

♪ Change the lyrics to suit a chosen activity, such as, "She likes to shop... every day..."

4. Let's All Play Together

Goal areas

- Communication skills: *Receptive language*
- Social/emotional skills: *Turn-taking*

Materials

- Guitar
- Assorted percussion instruments
- Music for "Let's All Play Together" by Kelly Summer (See Appendix A)

Activity

Sing the song "Let's All Play Together" to encourage group members to play their instruments at the appropriate time. Begin by having everyone play and stop as a group, then move to having specific group members play by themselves.

Notes

♪ This song utilizes the universal Blues progression and can be modified to any key as desired by the group facilitator.

♪ Create different playing groups by setting parameters such as "all ladies play" or "everyone wearing red can play."

5. Scarf Dance

Goal areas

- Sensorimotor: *Gross motor, Sensory integration*
- Leisure skills: *Imagination / creativity*

Materials

- Recording of various musical selections
- Scarves in a variety of colors

Activity

Make sure the group is sitting or standing in a circle. Give each group member a turn to choose a scarf or scarves (multiple scarves can be tied together and held with one hand) and dance in the center of the circle. Put on music to which that person freely dances. Encourage the dancer to interact with others in the group while dancing by approaching them to make eye contact, etc. Also encourage the seated group members to actively support the dancer by applauding, etc.

Notes

♪ Form pairs of participants to dance together. This may ease some shyness about dancing in the middle of the group.

6. I'm in the Mood

Goal areas

- Communication skills: *Expressive language*
- Sensorimotor: *Gross motor*
- Leisure skills: *Imagination/creativity*

Materials

- Guitar or piano (optional)
- Music for "I'm in the Mood" by Minako Kamimura (See Appendix A)

Activity

Sing the song "I'm in the Mood," giving every participant a chance to describe what they are in the mood to do and replacing the action word with the action of their choice. Instruct the group to choose simple things to do that can be done in that moment. Some examples include clapping, stomping, stretching, smiling, etc.

Notes

♪ Instead of gestures or movements, name various instruments that the participants are holding and ask whoever is holding the named instrument to play during that verse.

7. The Weekend Song

Goal areas

- Communication skills: *Expressive language, Initiating contact and communication*
- Cognitive skills: *Reality orientation, Memory*

Materials

- Guitar or piano
- Music for "The Weekend Song" by Maria Ramey (See Appendix A)

Activity

Sing "The Weekend Song" to each group member to prompt a recollection of what he did over the weekend.

Notes

♪ The past-tense wording of the song may be modified to ask what group members will do during an upcoming weekend.

♪ "Weekend" may be replaced by any day of the week (i.e., "What did you do on Monday?").

8. You Are My Sunshine

Goal areas

- Communication skills: *Expressive language*
- Cognitive skills: *Analyzing, Reality orientation*
- Social/emotional skills: *Identify/appropriately express emotion*

Materials

- Guitar or piano
- Music for "You Are My Sunshine" by Oliver Hood

Activity

Sing the first verse to the song "You Are My Sunshine." Discuss the lyrics, guiding the group to the realization that the "sunshine" referred to in the song is someone who makes the singer happy when she is feeling sad. Ask group members who their "sunshine" is. Who makes them happy when they are feeling sad? Sing the song again for each participant, substituting her chosen person's name for "sunshine" throughout the song until the end, when the standard lyrics "Please don't take my sunshine away" are sung.

Notes

♪ For a similar, more involved activity to be used with higher-functioning participants, see Activity 78, "You Are."

9. Triangle Teams

Goal areas

- Communication skills: *Initiating contact and communication*
- Sensorimotor: *Gross motor, Fine motor*
- Social/emotional skills: *Teamwork*

Materials

- Triangles, with loop or other way to hold it up, and beaters

Activity

Pair up group members and give each pair a triangle and beater. Instruct one team to play once on their triangle, emphasizing the teamwork involved in one person holding up the triangle and the other person hitting the triangle. Then the next pair may play once on their triangle. Continue until all pairs have played once. Repeat, going faster each time.

Notes

♪ Try having the pairs play twice or three times each.

♪ Point randomly to teams to play their triangles.

♪ For greater difficulty, ask one pair to play a unique rhythm on their triangle, which the other teams must copy.

10. Shaking to the Music Beat

Goal areas

- Communication skills: *Initiating contact and communication*
- Social/emotional skills: *Other*

Materials

- Guitar or piano
- Egg shakers
- Music for "I've Been Working on the Railroad," an American Folk Song

Activity

Make sure the group is sitting in a circle. Ask for a volunteer or designate someone to go first. Give this person two egg shakers and have him stand in the middle of the circle. Instruct him to choose a partner to give the second egg shaker to, in an invitation to join him in the middle of the circle. Once two people are standing in the circle, use the tune for the verse "Someone's in the kitchen with Dinah" from "I've Been Working on the Railroad," and sing the following, replacing the underlined names as appropriate:

> John is in the circle with Marcie, John is the one we'll me-ee-eet. John is in the circle with Marcie, shakin' to the music beat. Singing fee, fi fiddly-i-oh, fee, fi fiddly-i-oh-oh-oh-oh, fee, fi, fiddly-i-oh, shakin' to the music beat.

Have the second person then choose a new partner. Continue until everyone has had a chance to be "introduced" to the group.

Notes

- ♪ This activity is especially useful when introducing new members to a group.
- ♪ Encourage the group that is still sitting to sing and clap along.

11. Live Music Relaxation

Goal areas

- Communication skills: *Auditory perception*
- Leisure skills: *Relaxation*

Materials

- Assorted instruments with a "relaxing" sound to them. These may include a xylophone, ocean drum, rainstick, egg shakers, finger cymbals, wind chimes, etc.
- Guitar

Activity

Have the group sit in a circle and actively focus on breathing and relaxing their body. Instruct participants to choose an instrument that appeals to them based on whether it sounds/feels relaxing to them. Begin playing soft basic chords on the guitar and encourage participants to join in improvising as they feel ready, keeping the music soft, slow and relaxing. Remind the group to continue focusing on breathing and relaxing their body. Continue until the group seems relaxed.

Notes

♪ After the improvisation, discuss what the experience was like to both play and hear parts of the relaxing music within a group.

12. Shake up High

Goal areas

- Communication skills: *Receptive language*
- Sensorimotor: *Gross motor, Fine motor*
- Leisure skills: *Imagination/creativity*

Materials

- Shakers or other very small percussion instruments for each participant
- Guitar
- Music for "If You're Happy and You Know It," a traditional Latvian folk song

Activity

Pass the shakers out, then sing/play the song "If You're Happy and You Know It" and substitute ways to shake the shakers in place of "clap your hands." For example:

> "If you're happy and you know it, shake <u>up high</u> (down low/to the left/to the right/very loud/etc.). If you're happy and you know it, <u>shake up high</u>. If you're happy and you know it, let your shaker really show it, if you're happy and you know it, shake <u>up high</u>!"

Ask participants for suggestions on other ways to shake the shaker, encouraging them to be highly creative and adventurous with their suggestions.

Notes

♪ Small percussion instruments may be used instead of shakers. Sing "....play up high" and "...let your music really show it."

♪ Practice shaking the shakers up high, down low, etc. before actually beginning the song in order to introduce the concept to the group.

♪ A shaker can easily be held in your strumming hand while strumming, ready to be used at the appropriate times in order to physically demonstrate each way to shake that is sung.

13. Visual Lyric Analysis

Goal areas

- Communication skills: *Expressive language*
- Academic skills: *Reading*
- Cognitive skills: *Sequencing, Attention span*
- Leisure skills: *Music appreciation*

Materials

- Book illustrating a well-known folk song (See Appendix B for suggestions)
- Guitar or piano (optional)
- Recording of the chosen song (optional)

Activity

Sing the chosen song and ask for feedback on what group members think the song is about. Show the book to the group and tell them that they are going to learn what the words mean. Read through the book, discussing both the words and the accompanying pictures in detail. Sing the song again, turning the pages in the book so that everyone can follow along. Finish with a discussion about each participant's favorite part of the song (words or pictures) and/or whether the participants have a new understanding of what the song is about.

Notes

♪ Use a song that the group is familiar with.

♪ Using a recording of the song, or having an assistant play the song on guitar or piano, will facilitate the part of the activity when pages must be turned while singing. Alternatively, you may choose to sing a capella.

14. Cluster Drumming

Goal areas

- Social/emotional skills: *Teamwork, Impulse control*
- Leisure skills: *Imagination/creativity, Musical skill*

Materials

- Two to four Tubano drums or other tall drums
- Drum beaters
- Triangle with beater or similar distinctive-sounding instrument

Activity

Place multiple Tubano drums of various sizes together with a chair on either side of the drums. Choose two group members to sit in the chairs with drum beaters and play freely on the drums together. Play a triangle trill or other distinctive instrument to signal the end of the improvisation. Pass the drum beaters to the next pair of participants.

Notes

♪ Recordings of preferred music may be used as background.

♪ If the group is verbal, you may want to discuss each improvisation as a group.

15. Pick a Card: Instruments

Goal areas

- Social/emotional skills: *Turn-taking*

Materials

- Index cards with pictures of instruments drawn or printed on them
- Instruments to match the index cards
- Guitar (optional)

Activity

Ask a participant to draw a card. She must then find that instrument and play a solo on it while you support her with chord patterns on the guitar and/or while the group sings a short, familiar song. Give everyone a chance to draw a card.

Notes

♪ This activity can be paired with Activity 38, "Pick a Card: Feelings," with participants choosing one card from each set to portray the chosen emotion on the chosen instrument.

16. Frame Drum Imagination

Goal areas

- Cognitive skills: *Abstract thinking*
- Leisure skills: *Imagination/creativity*

Materials

- Frame drums for each group member

Activity

Pass out a frame drum to each member and encourage everyone to play along with a steady beat. Say, "Let's use our imaginations to pretend that these drums are something else. What kinds of things could they be?" Point out the round shape, size, depth, etc., as ways to stimulate ideas. When an idea is presented, have the entire group pretend as though the drums are that thing. For example, they might be cereal bowls: Pretend you are scooping up cereal from the drum in a spoon and eating it! Go back to playing a steady beat and ask the group to think of another thing the drum might represent. Continue acting out these things until everyone has had a chance to offer a suggestion.

Notes

♪ Some examples of things the drums may represent include bowls, steering wheels, cups, Ferris wheels, boats, hats, etc.

17. Heartbeat

Goal areas

- Leisure skills: *Relaxation*

Materials

- Buffalo drum, djembe or other drum with a warm tone
- A recording of calming music that is at a tempo of approximately 50 beats/minute

Activity

Encourage participants to become silent, relax and notice their own heartbeats. Play the drum in a slow and steady beat to simulate a calm heartbeat. Have participants join in by patting on their legs with the beat. After the group has become calm and in sync, instruct the participants to remain still and silent while you start the recorded music. As the recorded music plays, continue playing the "heartbeat" on the drum in sync with the music, allowing participants to either sit in silence as they "feel" the drumbeat or pat their legs along with the beat again.

Notes

- ♪ If participants are able, they may feel their own pulse on their wrists or necks.
- ♪ Consider adding the element of calm, improvised vocalizations with the music.
- ♪ Make sure to bring the group back up to a fully aware level following this activity, by having them stand up and stretch or increasing the tempo of the beat and segueing into a more upbeat improvisation using hand clapping and other body movements.

18. Over the Rainbow

Goal areas

- Cognitive skills: *Abstract thinking*
- Sensorimotor: *Gross motor, Sensory integration*
- Leisure skills: *Imagination/creativity, Music appreciation*

Materials

- Scarves in various colors
- Guitar or piano
- Music for the song "Over the Rainbow" by Harold Arlen and E.Y. Harburg

Activity

Pass out colored scarves, then introduce the song and demonstrate how a colorful rainbow can be created by sweeping a scarf in an arc above your head or in front of yourself. Sing the song "Over the Rainbow" while encouraging the participants to gracefully create rainbows all around the room.

Notes

♪ Encourage large, sweeping gestures to maximize physical movement/control.

♪ If physically and cognitively capable, pairs of participants may touch their scarves together and form a large arc together to mimic a multi-colored rainbow.

♪ See if the group can guess the song you're thinking of about rainbows, before you introduce the song.

19. I Love...

Goal areas

- Communication skills: *Expressive language*
- Cognitive skills: *Sequencing*
- Leisure skills: *Imagination/creativity, Music appreciation*

Materials

- Guitar or piano
- Dry-erase board, chalkboard or paper
- Marker, chalk or pencil
- Music for "I Love the Mountains" which is a traditional folk song

Activity

Sing the song "I Love the Mountains" then encourage a creative re-writing of the lyrics to make it more personal to the group. Ask for suggestions on what they love, write these things down and sing the song again with their chosen words.

Notes

♪ Be prepared with suggestions for participants with limited verbal skills. Ask if they enjoy certain things and include these things in the song if they nod or answer yes.

♪ Sing multiple verses to include everyone's suggestions, if necessary.

20. Old MacDonald Had a Band

Goal areas

- Cognitive skills: *Attention span*
- Sensorimotor: *Sensory integration*
- Social/emotional skills: *Impulse control*

Materials

- Assorted percussion instruments, a different one for each group member
- Guitar or piano
- Music for "Old MacDonald," a traditional folk song

Activity

Pass out instruments to the entire group and facilitate a discussion about what the instruments are called, how they are played and what they sound like. Tell the group that they are like a band and you are their leader. Then use the tune of "Old MacDonald" to sing the following, naming yourself and one of the instruments held by a group member:

> Mr./Miss Grayson had a band. Yes, oh yes he/she did. And in this band there was a tambourine, yes, oh yes there was. With a shake, shake here and a shake, shake there..., etc.

Encourage the group to listen when their instrument is named so that they can then play it. Continue until all instruments have been named.

Notes

♪ Sing about each instrument in the order they are held in the circle, then choose instruments randomly to increase the group's need to listen carefully in order to play at the right time.

♪ Decrease difficulty by only passing out three types of instruments, with multiple participants playing each type of instrument.

21. Clap Your Hands, One Two Three

Goal areas

- Communication skills: *Receptive language*
- Sensorimotor: *Gross motor, Sensory integration*

Materials

- Guitar or piano
- Music for "Clap Your Hands, One Two Three" by Minako Kamimura (See Appendix A)

Activity

Sing the song "Clap Your Hands, One Two Three" to each group member, encouraging them to clap their hands or perform other gestures you might sing, such as "stomp your feet," "touch your nose," "tap your head," etc.

Notes

♪ Instead of gestures, you may use percussion instruments and sing, "hit the drum," "ring the bell," etc.

22. I Feel Good

Goal areas

- Communication skills: *Expressive language*
- Cognitive skills: *Reality orientation*
- Social/emotional skills: *Identify/appropriately express emotion, Turn-taking*
- Leisure skills: *Imagination/creativity*

Materials

- Guitar or piano
- Music for "I Feel Good" by James Brown

Activity

Begin the activity by singing the song "I Feel Good." Give every group member a turn at personalizing the song by asking them, "How are you feeling today?" Use each participant's chosen feeling in the chorus of the song to replace the word *good*. Encourage the entire group to sing the song dramatically each time, acting out the feeling being expressed. For example, if participants say they feel tired, sing the song very slowly and encourage the group to yawn, close their eyes, snore, etc. This will enhance participation and promote a deeper connection with various feelings expressed.

Notes

- ♪ Encourage participants to respond with words that are more descriptive than "good" or "fine," or are different than words that others have already said.
- ♪ It may be helpful to display a list of descriptive feeling words that group members can choose from to express how they are feeling.

23. Matching Loud and Soft

Goal areas

- Communication skills: *Auditory perception*
- Cognitive skills: *Attention span*
- Social/emotional skills: *Impulse control*

Materials

- Loud percussion instruments (e.g., paddle drum, tambourine)
- Soft percussion instruments (e.g., triangle, shakers)

Activity

Assign loud instruments to half of the group and soft instruments to the other half. Play and sing a familiar song and vary the loudness or softness of the singing/playing spontaneously. Group members with soft instruments play only when the song gets soft, while members with loud instruments play only when the song gets loud.

Notes

♪ This activity can be simplified or taught by assigning a loud instrument to one person and a soft instrument to one person. Other group members may then take turns with the instruments.

♪ Add a secondary element of listening for and following by playing fast or slow.

24. Just for Fun

Goal areas

- Communication skills: *Initiating contact and communication*
- Cognitive skills: *Reality orientation, Memory*
- Social/emotional skills: *Turn-taking, Other*

Materials

- Guitar or piano
- Music for "Just for Fun" by Maria Ramey (See Appendix A)

Activity

Sing the song "Just for Fun" about yourself as a way to introduce the activity. Then take turns asking each person in the group what they like to do for fun. Sing the song for each person. Between participants, encourage memory and recall by randomly asking other group members to recall what previous participants said they liked to do for fun.

Notes

♪ If there are non-verbal participants in the group, be prepared to suggest a fun activity that you know they like to do.

♪ This activity is a good way to introduce new members to a group and to encourage participants to get to know more about each other.

25. Paint the Air

Goal areas

- Communication skills: *Auditory perception*
- Academic skills: *Other*
- Cognitive skills: *Abstract thinking, Analyzing*
- Sensorimotor: *Gross motor, Sensory integration*
- Leisure skills: *Imagination/creativity, Relaxation*

Materials

- Recording of relaxing, "colorful" instrumental music
- Shakers in various colors
- Scarves in various colors

Activity

Listen to the music and ask the group to imagine what colors the music might paint in the air if the sounds were colors. Discuss the colors the participants imagined and pass out shakers and scarves to match the colors they each chose. Listen to the song again while "painting" the air with color and sounds by waving the scarves and playing the shakers, moving in rhythm to the music.

Notes

♪ Encourage humming and vocalizations to fit the music as well.

♪ Encourage the painting of specific shapes in the air or of abstract brush strokes.

26. Howl at the Moon

Goal areas

- Communication skills: *Receptive language, Expressive language*
- Sensorimotor: *Gross motor*
- Social/emotional skills: *Turn-taking, Teamwork*

Materials

- Guitar or piano
- Music for "Howl at the Moon" by Kelly Summer (See Appendix A)

Activity

Sing "Howl at the Moon" with each participant taking a turn at replacing the words "stomp your feet" with an action of their choice. Have the group then participate in the action specified. For example, if someone sings "Gonna rock you 'till you <u>dance</u>!", encourage everyone to dance. During the words of the chorus "Gonna howl at the moon" and "Gonna howl like the wind," encourage the group to vocalize a howling or "ooh" sound.

Notes

♪ Be prepared with ideas for various actions. Some suggestions may include dance, clap, stomp, sway, tap, smile, cheer, etc.

27. Twelve Days

Goal areas

- Academic skills: *Counting/Math, Other*
- Cognitive skills: *Sequencing, Memory*
- Social/emotional skills: *Turn-taking*

Materials

- Guitar or piano
- Music for "Twelve Days of Christmas," a traditional English Christmas carol

Activity

Choose a season or holiday and ask group members to think of things related to that season/holiday that might be given as a gift, even if it would be a silly gift. Using the tune "Twelve Days of Christmas" (Traditional), sing a song about these gifts, adding each gift one at a time by asking the next group member to name another gift. For example:

> "On the first day of <u>summer</u>, my true love gave to me, <u>a swimming pool for my backyard</u>. On the second day of <u>summer</u>, my true love gave to me, <u>two beach balls</u> and <u>a swimming pool for my backyard</u>," etc.

Notes

- ♪ "Twelve Days of Halloween" could be played in a minor key.
- ♪ A board or large piece of paper may be used to write the named gifts down to assist with recall and encourage reading skills.

28. Random Duet

Goal areas

- Communication skills: *Auditory perception*
- Sensorimotor: *Gross motor, Sensory integration*
- Social/emotional skills: *Impulse control*

Materials

- Two small percussion instruments with unique sounds (e.g., tambourine and triangle)
- Guitar or piano
- Recorded music (optional)

Activity

Position the group in a close circle within easy reaching distance of each other. Give the two instruments to participants on opposite sides of the group. Start the music (either an improvisation on guitar or a recording) and instruct the group to keep passing the instruments to their right until the music stops. Stop the music randomly. When the music stops, the two people left holding the instruments must play a duet together. Accompany this duet on guitar or piano.

Notes

♪ Encourage eye contact between the duet players.

♪ This activity may also be done without accompaniment for the duet players.

29. Emotion Connection

Goal areas

- Communication skills: *Auditory perception, Expressive language*
- Social/emotional skills: *Identify/appropriately express emotion*

Materials

- Paper or flashcards with printed faces showing various emotions
- Various percussion instruments

Activity

Ask a participant to choose a particular feeling and play how that feeling would sound on an instrument of his choice. A second person must then choose the correct emotion displayed on a matching flashcard. Have various pairs of participants participate in this.

Notes

♪ Keep the interaction non-verbal to emphasize the use of non-verbal emotion cues.

♪ Another activity using these cards is Activity 38, "Pick a Card: Feelings."

30. Stretchy Band Hokey Pokey

Goal areas

- Communication skills: *Receptive language*
- Academic skills: *Other*
- Sensorimotor: *Gross motor, Sensory integration*
- Social/emotional skills: *Teamwork*
- Leisure skills: *Imagination/creativity*

Materials

- Stretchy band
- Music for "The Hokey Pokey," a traditional folk song

Activity

Sit in a circle and have everyone hold on to the stretchy band with both hands. Sing "The Hokey Pokey," filling in the blanks with body parts suggested by the group members. Instead of singing "turn yourself around," sing "turn the band around," and have the group turn the band in either a clockwise or counter-clockwise direction. For example:

> "You put your <u>head</u> in; you put your <u>head</u> out. You put your <u>head</u> in and you shake it all about. You do the hokey pokey and *you turn the band around.* That's what it's all about!"

Notes

♪ Practice turning the stretchy band around in a circle both clockwise and counter-clockwise before doing it with the song.

♪ Encourage color recognition by having clients identify the color they are holding onto when the song stops. Identify various objects in the room that match the color being identified.

31. Concerto Soloist

Goal areas

- Communication skills: *Auditory perception*
- Cognitive skills: *Attention span*
- Social/emotional skills: *Turn-taking, Teamwork, Impulse control*
- Leisure skills: *Imagination/creativity, Musical skill*

Materials

- Xylophone or other melodic instrument
- Assorted small percussion instruments such as shakers, maracas or tambourines

Activity

Explain to the group that a *concerto soloist* is, for example, "the person who gets to stand up in front of the orchestra and play something flashy while the whole orchestra follows along. The orchestra has to match the way the soloist is playing." Have group members take turns being the "soloist" on a xylophone or other melodic instrument. Instruct everyone else in the group to listen carefully to the tempo (speed) and dynamics (volume), and follow along on their percussion instruments to provide the backup orchestra.

Notes

♪ Demonstrate by playing the xylophone in various tempi and dynamics, prompting everyone to follow along and match/support the solo line.

32. Conducting

Goal areas

- Cognitive skills: *Sequencing, Abstract thinking, Attention span*
- Social/emotional skills: *Turn-taking, Teamwork*
- Leisure skills: *Music appreciation*

Materials

- Recording of slow, quiet, instrumental music
- Chimes or resonating bells

Activity

Have group members take turns being the conductor while everyone else plays a chime or resonating bell. Have the "conductor" stand in the middle of the circle or in front of the group. Start the CD and ask the conductor to point at different people to cue them to play their chimes. When the conductor waves both arms, everyone is to play. When the conductor stops, everyone must stop playing.

Notes

♪ The conductor can show changes in volume or tempo.

♪ Non-pitched percussion instruments can be substituted for the chimes or bells.

33. Guess the Hidden Instrument

Goal areas

- Cognitive skills: *Abstract thinking, Analyzing*
- Sensorimotor: *Sensory integration*

Materials

- Assorted small percussion instruments
- Scarves

Activity

Wrap an instrument in a scarf and pass the instrument around the group. Let participants touch, feel, shake or strike it, and ask if they can identify the instrument without seeing it. Try again with another instrument.

Notes

♪ Timing how long it takes to guess the right instrument can be a fun, competitive game.

♪ Instead of in a scarf, the instrument can be hidden in a box.

♪ Pictures of possible instruments with their names may assist participants in finding the answer.

34. How Many Beats?

Goal areas

- Communication skills: *Auditory perception, Receptive language*
- Academic skills: *Counting/Math*
- Cognitive skills: *Sequencing, Memory, Attention span*
- Social/emotional skills: *Turn-taking, Impulse control*

Materials

- A large djembe or conga drum

Activity

Have the group sit in a very close circle with the large drum placed in the middle. Using the drum to accompany yourself, improvise a simple tune and sing:

> "Everyone play the drum with me, repeat after me, repeat after me.
> Joshua play the drum with me, repeat after me, repeat after me." Create
> a simple rhythm on the drum and count it out loud: "One, two, three..."

Lean the drum toward the person named and allow them to copy your rhythm while saying, "One, two, three." Bring the drum back to yourself and sing another rhythm, e.g., "One, two, three, four, five." Create three or four different rhythms for that participant to copy. Sing the song again, naming a new participant, and continue until everyone has had a turn.

Notes

♪ Increase or decrease difficulty to match each participant's ability by creating a variety of rhythms, incorporating loud/soft dynamics and varying the tempo or number of beats played.

♪ To increase attention span, sing quickly and randomly choose a participant from the circle, playing just one rhythm then leaning the drum toward the chosen participant without naming them beforehand. This will require everyone to listen carefully to the rhythm, in case they are chosen to copy it.

35. Walkin' Down the Street

Goal areas

- Sensorimotor: *Gross motor, Sensory integration*
- Social/emotional skills: *Turn-taking, Teamwork*
- Leisure skills: *Imagination/creativity*

Materials

- Music for, or a recording of, "Do Wah Diddy Diddy" by Jeff Barry and Ellie Greenwich, as recorded by Manfred Mann
- Guitar or piano, if live music is used
- Ample space to move in

Activity

Have the group stand up and form a circle. Warm up by playing or singing the song "Do Wah Diddy Diddy" and encouraging movement to the music, such as walking in place, snapping fingers, shuffling feet, etc. Next, explain that everyone will have a chance to show the group how they can walk with style by walking creatively across the circle when it's their turn. Choose a volunteer or designate the first participant to walk across the circle as everyone sings the song again. Encourage the person walking across to sing, "Do wah diddy diddy dum diddy do" alone at the appropriate time in the lyrics. Continue until everyone has had a turn, making sure to clap and cheer for each person once they've crossed the circle.

Notes

♪ Group members who are unable to walk across the room unassisted may be pushed in a wheelchair while they move their arms creatively, or they may sit in a chair in the middle of the circle moving to the music or playing an instrument.

36. Walk Like the Music

Goal areas

- Communication skills: *Receptive language*
- Sensorimotor: *Gross motor*

Materials

- An assortment of various recorded musical selections
- Ample space to move in

Activity

Encourage participants to walk in a circle. Play short selections from assorted types of music and call out different kinds of "walks" appropriate to those musical selections. Encourage creativity and experimentation, making this a fun activity with lots of laughter and energetic movement.

Notes

♪ Compile songs in advance to minimize breaks in the flow. Create a playlist on a digital music player, or burn specific songs to CD in a planned order.

♪ Examples of some musical selections and related actions include: "Baby Elephant Walk" (Henry Mancini) – walk like an elephant; "Olympic Fanfare and Theme" (John Williams) – run in slow motion; "Locomotion" (Gerry Goffin/Carole King) – move like a train; and "Hot, Hot, Hot" (Alphonsus Cassell) – create a conga line.

♪ Adapt this activity for non-ambulatory participants by having the leader or an assistant push wheelchairs, or having participants stay seated in chairs and perform the requested motions with their arms.

37. Visual CDs

Goal areas

- Communication skills: *Expressive language*
- Cognitive skills: *Abstract thinking, Analyzing*
- Social/emotional skills: *Identify/appropriately express emotions, Turn-taking*
- Leisure skills: *Imagination/creativity, Music appreciation*

Materials

- CDs in jewel cases with original cover artwork/pictures showing. These should be obscure CDs not easily identified by the group, preferably with creative/unique artwork on the cover
- CD player

Activity

Place the CDs where the artwork can be seen easily. Give each group member a turn to choose a CD and share with the group why they chose that particular CD. Ask the group to guess what kind of music will be on the chosen CD (possible answers may include "rock," "country," "happy," "sad," "slow" or "fast,"), based on what the CD cover looks like. Play a selection from the chosen CD then ask the group how the music sounded and whether it was what they expected.

Notes

♪ For non-verbal or limited language participants, ask simple yes/no questions that they may answer (e.g., "Is the music fast?").

♪ Encourage participants to find a CD with a blue cover, red cover, with a bird in the picture, etc. to stimulate interest and expand this activity.

38. Pick a Card: Feelings

Goal areas

- Social/emotional skills: *Identify/appropriately express emotion, Turn-taking*

Materials

- Index cards with emotions written on them or faces printed or drawn on them to portray various emotions (e.g., angry, happy, sad, sleepy, surprised, etc.)
- Assorted instruments

Activity

Ask a participant to select a card at random. She must then choose an instrument on which to "play" the depicted feeling. Have the rest of the group guess what the feeling being depicted might be and discuss what clues were, or were not, in the music regarding the feeling.

Notes

♪ Encourage participants to be very dramatic in their portrayals of each feeling, using body language and facial expression to help portray the feeling. Point out various non-verbal cues to the rest of the group, telling them they are clues as to what the feeling is.

♪ This activity can be paired with Activity 15, "Pick a Card: Instruments," with participants choosing one card from each set to portray the chosen emotion on the chosen instrument.

♪ These cards may also be used for Activity 29, "Emotion Connection."

39. Jump and Jive

Goal areas

- Communication skills: *Auditory perception*
- Sensorimotor: *Gross motor, Sensory integration*

Materials

- Recorded instrumental selections in various musical styles (e.g., Swing, Big Band, relaxing music)
- Lightweight ankle or wrist weights (optional)

Activity

Begin the activity with warm-up stretches using a slow, recorded selection. Encourage participants to move their arms and legs in sync with the musical beat. Demonstrate various movements and ask for creative examples from participants as well. Gradually increase physical tempo and energy by putting on selections of increasing tempo and energy. Bring the activity to a close by returning to a slow, meditative musical selection.

Notes

♪ Be aware of the range of motion for each participant and make necessary adjustments.

♪ Add ankle or wrist weights to create a more intense exercise experience, if appropriate.

40. Mirroring

Goal areas

- Communication skills: *Initiating contact and communication*
- Cognitive skills: *Attention span*
- Sensorimotor: *Gross motor*
- Social/emotional skills: *Turn-taking, Impulse control*
- Leisure skills: *Imagination/creativity*

Materials

- Recorded instrumental music

Activity

Demonstrate various movements and encourage group members to copy them to warm up. For example, move like a tree blowing in the wind, a person painting a mural or make animal movements. Pair up group members and have them sit or stand facing each other, encouraging eye contact. Allow each pair to choose who will lead the first round. Begin the music and instruct the "leaders" to move in creative ways while their partner mirrors the leader and copies their movements. After sufficient time has passed, instruct everyone to switch leaders.

Notes

♪ Process this experience by discussing things like what it felt like to lead, what it felt like to follow and whether eye contact was helpful in focusing on the leader.

41. Twist

Goal areas

- Sensorimotor: *Gross motor, Fine motor*
- Social/emotional skills: *Turn-taking*
- Leisure skills: *Imagination/creativity*

Materials

- Music for, or a recording of, the song "Twist" by Hank Ballard, as recorded by Chubby Checker
- Guitar or piano, if live music is used

Activity

Play and sing the song "Twist" and encourage the group to stand up and twist back and forth as appropriate to the lyrics. Ask group members for suggestions on different ways to twist, and instruct everyone to copy them.

Notes

♪ Some ways to "twist" might include twisting the upper body back and forth, turning in a circle, rolling fists or arms around each other, turning the ankle/foot back and forth, twirling hair or twisting fingers together.

42. Follow My Beat

Goal areas

- Communication skills: *Auditory perception*
- Cognitive skills: *Sequencing, Memory, Attention span*
- Sensorimotor: *Sensory integration*
- Social/emotional skills: *Turn-taking*
- Leisure skills: *Musical skill*

Materials

- Paddle or hand drums for every person in the group

Activity

Introduce the concept of rhythmic beats by beating the syllables of every group member's name on a drum while dramatically saying that person's name. Encourage the group to copy the rhythms, then make up a simple rhythm that the group will copy. Have each group member then take a turn at creating a beat for the rest of the group to copy.

Notes

♪ If drums are not available, this activity can easily be done with hand clapping.

43. My Favorite Things

Goal areas

- Communication skills: *Expressive language*
- Cognitive skills: *Sequencing, Reality orientation, Memory*
- Social/emotional skills: *Identify/appropriately express emotion*

Materials

- Guitar
- Music for "My Favorite Things" from *The Sound of Music* by Richard Rodgers and Oscar Hammerstein
- Dry/erase board and markers, or pre-printed sheets with blanks listed for each syllable of the song

Activity

Sing the song "My Favorite Things" from *The Sound of Music*. Facilitate a discussion of why this song was sung in the original musical (as a way to take your mind off of something scary) and how this could be a useful tool. Ask group members what some of their favorite things are. List these on the board or fill in the lyric blanks on a pre-printed sheet. Then sing the song again, substituting their suggestions instead of the original lyrics, where appropriate. Depending on the size of the group and amount of time available, you may choose to just rewrite one verse or multiple verses.

Notes

♪ Try to arrange suggestions in an order that will line up syllables with the original syllables to make singing the new version easy. This can be made easier by creating a pre-printed sheet of paper with blanks representing each syllable to be filled.

♪ Read the activities back to the group before singing the song to encourage memory retention.

♪ Sing this new version of the song multiple times (slowly) to give group members several opportunities to recall the favorite activities listed by the group.

44. Cha, Cha, Cha

Goal areas

- Communication skills: *Receptive language*
- Cognitive skills: *Attention span*
- Social skills: *Impulse control*

Materials

- Guitar or piano
- Assorted percussion instruments
- Music for "Cha Cha Cha" by Kihoko Moriwaki (See Appendix A)

Activity

Make sure every group member has a percussion instrument to play, then sing the song "Cha Cha Cha" with participants playing and singing the "cha, cha, cha" rhythm.

Notes

♪ Consider having each participant taking a turn playing the rhythm alone while you sing the song.

45. Signs of the Seasons

Goal areas

- Communication skills: *Expressive language*
- Cognitive skills: *Sequencing, Reality orientation*

Materials

- Guitar or piano
- Music for "When the Saints Go Marching In" by Virgil Stamps

Activity

Choose a season and facilitate a discussion of what the particular signs are of that season (weather, food, clothing, holidays, etc.). Have group members take turns inserting appropriate phrases to replace the underlined words in the following song, sung to the tune of "When the Saints Go Marching In":

"Oh when it's time to swim in pools. Oh when it's time to swim in pools. Yes we will know that it is summer when it is time to swim in pools."

Notes

♪ Add gestures or instrument sounds to go along with the singing.

46. Manic Monday

Goal areas

- Communication skills: *Expressive language*
- Cognitive skills: *Sequencing, Reality orientation, Memory*

Materials

- Music for the chorus of "Manic Monday" by Prince, as recorded by The Bangles
- Guitar or piano

Activity

This activity is best done on a Monday. Ask if anyone can name the day of the week, then give each group member a turn to share how their day feels (e.g., good, boring, happy, sleepy, etc.) and also recall what they did yesterday/on Sunday (e.g., watched TV, had dinner with friends, etc.). Once a participant has shared, sing the chorus of "Manic Monday," filling in the blanks as demonstrated below:

> "It's just another <u>sleepy</u> Monday. I wish it was Sunday. 'Cause <u>I</u> <u>watched TV, I had dinner with friends</u>. It's just another <u>sleepy</u> Monday."

Continue until everyone has had a turn to fill in the blanks.

Notes

- ♪ The song may also be modified to be used on a different day of the week, substituting the correct days of the week for the current day and recalled day.
- ♪ Listing participants' answers on a board may help the group remember what each person said and may enhance reading skills.

47. News from Home

Goal areas

- Communication skills: *Expressive language, Initiating contact and communication*
- Cognitive skills: *Reality orientation*
- Social/emotional skills: *Identify/appropriately express emotion, Turn-taking*

Materials

- Various recorded instrumental music selections, preferably recognizable to the participants
- Microphone (optional)

Activity

Tell the group they will be participating in a pretend radio show. They will each be sharing their news from home. Choose a volunteer or designate someone to go first. He may choose music appropriate to the news he is about to share, which you will set to play softly in the background while he speaks on the microphone. Once that person has shared his news from home (e.g., what he did over the weekend, something exciting he's looking forward to, etc.), he may then choose someone else to go next and share her news from home.

Notes

♪ Consider setting a time limit for each person's news spot just as someone on the radio or television would do. This will help keep things from running too long.

48. Traveling Places

Goal areas

- Academic skills: *Other*
- Cognitive skills: *Abstract thinking*
- Leisure skills: *Imagination / creativity*

Materials

- Guitar or piano
- Maps or a globe (optional)
- Music for "La Raspa/Mexican Hat Dance," a traditional Mexican folk song

Activity

Give group members a turn to pick a city, state or country that they would like to visit. Using the opening phrase of the tune to "La Raspa," sing the following, inserting the name of the chosen destination at the end of the song:

> "Ole, ole, ole. Come on everyone, let's go! Away, away, away. We're going to Mexico!"

Discuss what the participants know about their chosen destinations, why they want to go there, what they would do when they go there and what they might see or hear.

Notes

♪ Using maps, images or a world globe may be helpful in stimulating destination ideas.

49. Colors Everywhere

Goal areas

- Academic skills: *Other*
- Cognitive skills: *Attention span*

Materials

- Colored scarves
- Guitar or piano
- Music for "Colors Everywhere" by Maria Ramey (See Appendix A)

Activity

Pass out colored scarves to all group members, including as wide a variety of colors as possible. Sing the song "Colors Everywhere," going in a circle and having participants call out the colors they are holding when it comes to their turn. Do this multiple times, going faster each time. Once this become easy, have participants switch scarves so that everyone holds a new color, and repeat. Discuss how colorful the world is and ask for examples of the various colors in nature.

Notes

♪ Before beginning the song portion of the activity, it may be helpful to have participants name the colors they are holding and identify various objects, like fruits, that match that color.

♪ This activity is easily followed by Activity 18, "Over the Rainbow."

50. Nature Box

Goal areas

- Sensorimotor: *Sensory integration*
- Leisure skills: *Imagination/creativity, Relaxation*

Materials

- Recorded music including nature sounds, such as ocean waves, whales, birds, crickets or rain
- A box filled with nature items such as seashells, small sticks, pine cones, plastic fruit, flowers (real or plastic), small rocks, pieces of tree bark, straw, leaves, etc.

Activity

Begin playing the music and ask the group to imagine they are outside in a peaceful setting that is evoked by the music. Pass the box around or put it in the center of the group, and ask participants to choose an item from the box that they might expect to find in their peaceful place. Have the participants hold and feel these items, listening quietly to the music and imagining this peaceful place. After listening for a while, turn the volume down on the music and ask participants to share what they imagined and what made it seem peaceful for them.

Notes

♪ Many artificial nature items can be found at craft stores. These will last longer and create less mess; however, the real thing will feel and smell more authentic. Weigh these options according to your needs.

♪ Consider any participants' allergies to real nature items such as tree bark, leaves or flowers.

♪ If fruit is used, plastic is recommended, as participants may be tempted to eat the real thing!

♪ Instead of verbally describing their imagined peaceful place, consider having participants draw a representation of this place as the music continues.

51. This Is Me

Goal areas

- Communication skills: *Expressive language*
- Cognitive skills: *Analyzing*
- Social/emotional skills: *Self-esteem*

Materials

- Various instruments
- Guitar or piano (optional)

Activity

Have each group member take a turn describing herself in terms of both physical traits (tall, short, hair color, etc.) and personality traits (funny, nice, friendly, quiet, etc.), then ask the participant to choose an instrument to represent herself with all of those traits. Have her play this instrument while you verbally repeat those traits back to her. Once everyone has had a turn, initiate a group improvisation with everyone contributing their unique traits to the music. Discuss how everyone brings something special to the group.

Notes

♪ Participants often describe the things they like to do or eat, or places they go, etc., when asked to describe themselves, struggling with the concept of self-description. Stimulate ideas by having participants describe each other first.

♪ If participants have a history of negativity or low self-esteem, be prepared to redirect any negative descriptions or lay out parameters specifying that participants are not allowed to say anything negative about themselves (or others).

♪ You may want to also use a guitar or piano to improvise chord patterns to support each person as they play.

52. Wave the Scarves

Goal areas

- Communication skills: *Receptive language*
- Cognitive skills: *Sequencing, Attention span*
- Sensorimotor: *Gross motor, Sensory integration*

Materials

- Guitar or piano
- Assorted colored scarves
- Music for "Wave the Scarves" by Kihoko Moriwaki (See Appendix A)

Activity

Ask each group member to choose a scarf. Sing "Wave the Scarves" and have the group follow the directions in the song: wave the scarves up high/down low, toss and catch the scarves, spin them, blow them, etc.

Notes

♪ Ask participants to come up with more creative movements to do with the scarves.

53. Shake a Question

Goal areas

- Communication skills: *Auditory perception, Receptive language, Initiating contact and communication*
- Academic skills: *Other*
- Sensorimotor: *Gross motor, Sensory integration*
- Social/emotional skills: *Other*

Materials

- Two shakers, one red and one blue (or any other two distinctive colors)
- Recorded music

Activity

Make sure the group is in a close circle within easy reaching distance of each other. Give the two shakers to participants on opposite sides of the group. Start the music and instruct the group to keep passing the shakers to their right until the music stops. When the music stops randomly, the person holding the red shaker must ask a question of the person holding the blue shaker, or pay him a compliment or complete another predetermined social exchange.

Notes

♪ For a more complex activity, give everyone in the group a shaker while only having one red and one blue shaker in the mix. Have all shakers passed around the group while the music is playing. When the music stops, ask participants to look at their shakers to see whether they have one of the key colors.

54. Guess That Sound

Goal areas

- Communication skills: *Auditory perception*
- Cognitive skills: *Analyzing, Memory*
- Social/emotional skills: *Other*
- Leisure skills: *Musical skill*

Materials

- Included CD with various instrument sounds
- Instruments to match the instrument sounds you've chosen to play (e.g., shakers, tambourine, triangle, piano, guitar, maracas, jingle bells, paddle drum)
- Guitar or piano (optional)

Activity

Lay out the instruments in the middle of the circle so they can be seen by everyone. Play each instrument one at a time while instructing everyone to listen carefully and remember what they sound like. Play a chosen instrument sound from the CD and ask who knows which instrument it is to raise his hand. Call on the first raised hand, and if she has guessed correctly, give her the instrument and encourage her to give a short solo performance on the instrument while you accompany the solo with chord patterns on the guitar. Encourage cheering and clapping from the group. Continue until everyone has had a chance to guess and perform.

Notes

♪ Give everyone a chance to perform by asking that only those who have not yet played guess the instrument.

♪ To make this activity easier, allow the participants to experiment with the instruments to find the matching instrument sound.

♪ Record other instruments you may have that are not included on the enclosed CD.

55. Clap Your Hands to the Music

Goal areas

- Communication skills: *Receptive language*
- Cognitive skills: *Attention span*
- Sensorimotor: *Gross motor, Sensory integration*

Materials

- Guitar or piano
- Music for "Clap Your Hands to the Music" by Kihoko Moriwaki (See Appendix A)

Activity

Sing the song "Clap Your Hands to the Music," with participants clapping along. Replace "clap your hands" with other actions, such as "stomp your feet," "tap your knees," "tap your shoulders," "rub your tummy," etc.

Notes

♪ Use small percussion instruments to play with the music.

56. Move to the Music

Goal areas

- Communication skills: *Receptive language*
- Cognitive skills: *Attention span*
- Sensorimotor: *Gross motor, Sensory integration*
- Social/emotional skills: *Impulse control*

Materials

- Guitar or piano
- Jingle bells that can be wrapped around the ankle
- Music for "Move to the Music" by Kihoko Moriwaki (See Appendix A)

Activity

Put ankle bells on each person in the group. Have them then stand up and follow the directions in the song, "Move to the Music." When the song stops, everyone must sit in a chair.

Notes

♪ Vary the tempo of the song to vary dance style/movements.

♪ Create new verses to the song based on participants' abilities and the amount of room available.

♪ Non-ambulatory participants may have bells placed on/in their hands and be encouraged to make the motions with their hands.

57. Dance Conducting

Goal areas

- Cognitive skills: *Abstract thinking*
- Sensorimotor: *Gross motor, Sensory integration*
- Social/emotional skills: *Teamwork, Impulse control*
- Leisure skills: *Imagination/creativity*

Materials

- Various small percussion instruments, including a xylophone or other melodic instruments
- Scarves (optional)

Activity

Have the group sit in a large circle with ample space in the middle. Choose a volunteer or designate someone to stand in the center to be the dancer, while everyone else chooses an instrument to play. Ask the dancer to think of a kind of music he would like to dance to: slow/fast, loud/soft, flowing/jerky, etc. Instruct the dancer to move in ways that would match that type of music. The rest of the group must watch the dancer's movements and play music to match the movements on their instruments. Encourage dancers to be creative and change movements from time to time so that the instrumentalists can follow the changes. Have the dancer then choose a new person to be in the middle and conduct the group by dancing. Continue until everyone has had a turn.

Notes

♪ Participants in wheelchairs or who are otherwise non-ambulatory for this activity can still participate by sitting in the middle of the circle and moving their hands, head or feet to give the instrumentalists something to follow.

58. Marching In

Goal areas

- Communication skills: *Receptive language*
- Sensorimotor: *Gross motor*
- Social/emotional skills: *Turn-taking*
- Leisure skills: *Imagination/creativity*

Materials

- Guitar or keyboard
- Music for "When the Saints Go Marching In" by Virgil Stamps
- Ample room to move in

Activity

Have the group stand and sing/play the first verse of the song "When the Saints Go Marching In" while encouraging everyone to march in place. Ask one of the group members to choose a movement other than marching. Sing the song again, substituting the person's name for "the saints" and her chosen movement for "marching." Continue until all group members have had a turn.

Notes

♪ Some examples of movements include walking, swinging arms, clapping, dancing, tiptoeing, walking backwards, stomping or jumping.

♪ Participants in wheelchairs may be encouraged to use upper body movements and to substitute knee taps or arm movements for "marching" movements.

59. Song Bingo

Goal areas

- Academic skills: *Counting/Math*
- Cognitive skills: *Sequencing, Attention span*
- Sensorimotor: *Fine motor, Sensory integration*
- Leisure skills: *Music appreciation*

Materials

- Self-created "Bingo" sheets with nine songs printed within equal squares (each sheet containing the songs in different boxes). One sheet for each group member
- Nine slips of paper with the song names printed on them
- A bowl to draw from (optional)
- Colored pencils
- Guitar or piano

Activity

Have group members take turns randomly picking out a slip of paper with a song name printed on it. The group must then color in the square on their sheet which contains the name of the song, while singing the song. Repeat until someone in the group gets Bingo, which is three songs in a row horizontally, vertically or diagonally.

Notes

♪ Choose songs familiar to the group.

60. Musical Ball

Goal areas

- Communication skills: *Expressive language*
- Academic skills: *Reading*
- Cognitive skills: *Reality orientation, Memory*
- Sensorimotor: *Gross motor, Sensory integration*
- Social/emotional skills: *Impulse control*

Materials

- Recorded music or piano
- Medium-sized beach ball
- Questions written on slips of paper (these questions may be general, like "What is your favorite color?" or more in-depth, such as, "When was the last time you were really scared?")
- Bowl to draw slips of paper from

Activity

Have the group sit in a circle and either pass the ball around or toss it gently from one to another as the music plays. When the music stops, the group member holding the ball will be asked to draw a question from the bowl. Encourage the participants to read the question on their own, or you may read it for them. They must then answer their question. Continue until everyone has had an opportunity to draw and answer a question.

Notes

♪ Be prepared to stop the music when participants who have not yet answered a question are holding the ball. This will help ensure that everyone gets a chance.

61. Musical Feelings

Goal areas

- Communication skills: *Auditory perception, Expressive language*
- Social/emotional skills: *Identify/appropriately express emotion*

Materials

- Recordings of several instrumental selections representing various moods, such as angry, happy, playful, sad, mysterious, etc.
- Assorted melodic and percussive instruments

Activity

Play various musical selections and facilitate a discussion about what feelings are expressed in each selection of music. Suggest that the group then create their own music to represent a feeling. Encourage the group to come to a decision together about a specific feeling to express through music, then facilitate an improvisation on the chosen feeling.

Notes

♪ For a more complex activity, ask participants to share individual experiences when they felt each of the feelings represented by the musical selections.

♪ To improvise, you may choose to ask how someone might feel at a specific time, such as "when someone gives you a gift" or "when your friend won't talk to you."

62. Party Animal

Goal areas

- Communication skills: *Expressive language*
- Cognitive skills: *Abstract thinking*
- Social/emotional skills: *Other*
- Leisure skills: *Imagination/creativity*

Materials

- Various instruments with unique sounds (e.g., tambourine, maracas, paddle drum, chimes, cocorico, triangle)
- Guitar or piano

Activity

Have group members name and describe their favorite animals and choose instruments to represent that animal, based on shape, size, sound, personality, etc. Ask the group to imagine that the animals are all going to a party (for a birthday, holiday or other special event). Begin an improvisation in a major key, encouraging the group to verbally describe what their animals might do, eat, say or see at this party, and express this by playing their instruments. When the improvisation is finished, discuss what the animals were doing and how they might feel after the party. Optionally, play a second short improvisation to express how they would feel.

Notes

♪ For the improvisation, a simple repeated chord progression of I-IV-V-I is all that is needed in the tempo or style that fits the party or after-party feeling.

♪ Encourage participants to also act out what their chosen animals might do while playing their instrument, if appropriate.

63. Celebration Song

Goal areas

- Communication skills: *Expressive language*
- Cognitive skills: *Abstract thinking, Memory*
- Social/emotional skills: *Identify/appropriately express emotion*
- Leisure skills: *Imagination/creativity*

Materials

- Recording of a song from a movie known to the group which depicts a celebration scene
- Guitar or piano
- Assorted instruments

Activity

Play the recorded music and encourage a discussion of what the music depicts. Discuss the movie scene it is portraying and talk about what is being celebrated. Tell the group members that they will be writing their own celebration song and ask them to think about things they might want to celebrate. Ask group members what they would celebrate and have them choose instruments to represent the event or something that they would like to have at the celebration (i.e., cake, balloons, a swimming pool, etc.) and play that instrument briefly to demonstrate their celebration. Once all participants have had a turn to speak and choose an instrument, facilitate an improvisation to create some music that is celebratory in nature. Follow with a discussion about the song that was created and how it represented their celebration.

Notes

♪ During the improvisation, encourage and acknowledge participants individually by calling out their stated reasons to celebrate and/or things they would like to have at their celebration.

♪ Instead of a recorded song, you may sing a well-known celebratory song, such as that for a birthday or holiday.

64. Drum Q&A

Goal areas

- Communication skills: *Auditory perception, Initiating contact and communication*
- Social/emotional skills: *Turn-taking*

Materials

- Any type of drum

Activity

Have participants take turns choosing other people in the group to ask a question of. Those other people are then to "play" their answers on the drum instead of answering verbally. Have the group discuss and guess what the answer might be based on the drumming response. Ask the answering person to then share with the group what the answer really was.

Notes

♪ Consider having a selection of various kinds of drums for participants to choose according to what they would like their answer to sound like.

65. Rhythm Sticks Alphabet

Goal areas

- Academic skills: *Reading, Other*
- Cognitive skills: *Abstract thinking*

Materials

- Rhythm sticks
- Guitar or piano

Activity

Use rhythm sticks to form various letters of the alphabet, either by holding them in the air or arranging them on the floor or table. Ask the group to guess the letter, then elicit suggestions of words that start or end with that particular letter. Pass out rhythm sticks to the group to play along and sing a song that starts with that letter. This song can be either chosen by you or by the group.

Notes

♪ Writing down the letter or suggested words on paper, white board or a blackboard may assist with cognition, spelling and reading skills.

66. Your Story Through a Song

Goal areas

- Communication skills: *Expressive language*
- Cognitive skills: *Reality orientation*
- Social/emotional skills: *Turn-taking*
- Leisure skills: *Music appreciation*

Materials

- Various recorded song selections familiar to group members

Activity

Give each group member a turn to select a song from the recordings at hand. Instruct the participant to choose a song that represents something special (e.g., it may remind him of a favorite memory, describe a way he feels, etc.) but ask him not to say out loud just yet why that song is important to him. Once the group has listened to the song, ask the participant to explain why he chose that song. Encourage a discussion of how other group members may relate to what the participant has shared.

Notes

♪ You may choose to have participants share why they have chosen particular songs before the songs are played, so that the group may think about those reasons while they listen to the songs.

67. Five Letter Favorites

Goal areas

- Academic skills: *Reading, Other*
- Cognitive skills: *Sequencing, Abstract thinking*

Materials

- Guitar or piano (optional)
- Music for "B-I-N-G-O," a traditional folk song

Activity

Ask group members to identify favorite foods, instrument sounds, etc., which have five letters or can be spelled in five sections. Replace the underlined words in the following song sung to the tune of "B-I-N-G-O":

"There is a sound I like to hear and <u>drums</u> make that sound. <u>D-R-U-M-S</u>," etc.

OR

"There is a food I like to eat and <u>melon</u> tastes so good. <u>M-E-L-O-N</u>," etc.

Notes

♪ Some more examples of five-letter instruments include bells, flute, piano, snare, cello and banjo.

♪ Other examples of five-letter foods include candy, cakes, beans, apple, pears, fries, pasta, salad, bread and pizza.

♪ Some words can be spelled in five sections, such as "CH-I-M-E-S," without compromising the tune.

68. Boom Boom

Goal areas

- Cognitive skills: *Sequencing, Memory, Attention span*
- Social/emotional skills: *Turn-taking, Impulse control, Self-esteem*
- Leisure skills: *Imagination/creativity*

Materials

- Tambourine
- Music for "Boom Boom, Ain't it Great to Be Crazy," a traditional folk song

Activity

Have the group sit in a circle and begin by hitting the tambourine two times for "boom, boom" and singing a personalized version of the chorus from "Boom Boom, Ain't it Great to Be Crazy." Replace the word "crazy" with your name. When you sing your name, create a small dance movement that will represent you (e.g., throw your arms up). Ask the person next to you to then create a dance movement to represent herself. Have the entire group practice this dance move together, then hold the tambourine out to the new participant to hit it twice for "boom, boom" and sing the song using her name, encouraging everyone to perform the created dance move while singing that person's name. Continue around the circle until everyone has created their own personalized dance movements. Each time a new person has had a turn, repeat the song and dance movements for the participants who have already taken a turn, encouraging recall by the group of what dance movements were created.

Notes

♪ After everyone has had a turn, sing the song with random group members' names to test recollection of dance movement associations.

69. I Won't Back Down

Goal areas

- Communication skills: *Expressive language*
- Cognitive skills: *Reality orientation*
- Social/emotional skills: *Identify/appropriately express emotion*

Materials

- Music for, or a recording of, "I Won't Back Down" by Tom Petty
- Guitar or piano
- Dry-erase board, chalkboard or sheet of paper
- Marker, chalk or pen

Activity

Begin this activity with a discussion about what it means to "not back down" from something. Explain that it can mean not giving up when we face problems in life. Sing or play the recording of the song "I Won't Back Down." On the board or a sheet of paper, write "You can stand me up against _____ but I won't back down." Facilitate a discussion of some problems that group members may be facing in their lives. Ask volunteers to share particular problems that they face with the group, and to write those problems in the blanks on the board or paper. Provide help as needed. Sing the chorus to the song again, substituting the chosen problem. Continue with other group members who wish to share. Close with a positive discussion about not backing down from the problems that life throws at us.

Notes

♪ If a recording is being used, the group can still shout out the chosen problem when appropriate in the song.

70. Leadership: African Drumming

Goal areas

- Communication skills: *Receptive language, Initiating contact and communication*
- Social/emotional skills: *Turn-taking, Teamwork*
- Leisure skills: *Imagination/creativity, Musical skills, Music appreciation*

Materials

- Djembe drum
- Agogo bell
- Two shakers (preferably Hosho, made from hollowed gourds)
- Assorted drums and percussion instruments

Activity

Explain to the group that they will create an African Ensemble in this session. Introduce the instruments and explain that it is common for the leader of the African ensemble to play the drum in a certain way to indicate what dance moves the dancers should do. The Agogo bell is a common African instrument as well, as are shakers, called Hosho. Pass the instruments out and explain that the leader of the group will play the Djembe, counting to four before the group begins playing, and again counting to four, then saying "stop" when it is time to stop the music. The other members of the group are to follow the beat played on the Djembe on their own instruments. Play the Djembe first as an example, leading an improvisation. Then have participants stand up, place their instruments on their chair or the floor, and rotate one chair to the left so that they play new instruments. Continue until everyone has had a chance to play the Djembe and lead the group.

Notes

- ♪ If standing and changing chairs is difficult for members of the group, pass the instruments around the circle instead.
- ♪ A map may be used to allow the group to find Africa in relation to the continent they themselves are on.

71. Marching Band

Goal areas

- Communication skills: *Auditory perception, Receptive language*
- Sensorimotor: *Gross motor, Sensory integration*
- Social/emotional skills: *Turn-taking, Teamwork*
- Leisure skills: *Musical skill*

Materials

- Large paddle drum with mallet
- Various small percussion instruments such as drums, shakers or tambourines
- Music for "Who's in the Marching Band?" by Lindsay Felchle (See Appendix A)

Activity

Pass out various small percussion instruments, inviting everyone to stand up. Explain that you will be creating a marching band, and have the group members begin marching either in place or in a circle as you play the large paddle drum. Sing the song "Who's in the Marching Band?" and personalize it by inserting participants' names and instruments being played in place of the examples in the song. When you call out the names and instruments, encourage participants to play the correct rhythm with you on their instruments. Continue until everyone has had a turn.

Notes

♪ You may want to practice the rhythm before you start the song by having the group repeat the rhythm with and after you several times.

♪ There can be any number of people with the same instruments within the group. The included example of the song creates two spots to fill in with names, but this can be expanded to name everyone playing that instrument.

72. Eye Choose You

Goal areas

- Communication skills: *Initiating contact and communication*
- Cognitive skills: *Attention span*
- Social/emotional skills: *Other*

Materials

- Guitar (optional)
- Various percussion instruments

Activity

Make sure the group is seated in a circle, then facilitate a discussion about the importance of eye contact when conversing with someone else. Practice eye contact by encouraging each group member to maintain eye contact with you as you complete a small social exchange, such as "Hello, how are you today?" Explain that the group will play music together, but individuals can only join in and play when eye contact is made and they are given a silent invitation to join by a head nod. Begin playing the guitar (or other instrument) and look at group members one at a time to make eye contact, nodding your head to signal that they may join in the music. Continue until the entire group is playing, looking silently around the group and rewarding each new instance of eye contact with a smile.

Notes

♪ To make this activity more complex, instruct new participants to choose the next members to join by initiating eye contact and nodding at them. This will require all group members to notice the newest person and watch to see whether they will be chosen to play next, through silent eye contact and head nodding.

73. What I Like About You

Goal areas

- Communication skills: *Expressive language*
- Social/emotional skills: *Self-esteem*
- Leisure skills: *Imagination/creativity*

Materials

- Xylophone and mallets
- Assorted percussion instruments

Activity

Choose a volunteer or designate someone to go first. All other group members must say what they like about that person and choose instruments to musically express this trait by "playing it" on their instruments. Give the xylophone to the chosen person and ask him to say and play on the xylophone what he likes about himself. Have the rest of the group then join in on their instruments to play music with and for the chosen person, creating a serenade especially for that person, celebrating what great qualities he has. During the improvisation, restate the qualities that were identified. Once the improvisation is finished, ask the chosen person to then choose a new person whose likeable traits will be pointed out and played. Continue until everyone has had a turn.

Notes

♪ Be ready with suggestions for people who may get stuck trying to come up with compliments for others.

♪ Instruct group members to only choose someone who hasn't already had a turn.

♪ This activity can be done without the xylophone.

74. I Can See Clearly Now

Goal areas

- Communication skills: *Auditory perception, Receptive language*
- Cognitive skills: *Sequencing, Attention span*
- Social/emotional skills: *Impulse control*

Materials

- A recording of "I Can See Clearly Now" by Johnny Nash
- Rainstick/s
- Thundertube/s
- Tambourine/s (preferably yellow)
- Xylophone/s or a similar instrument
- Scarf or streamer

Activity

Begin with a discussion about the weather and specific elements that various weather conditions may have, such as rain, sunshine, rainbows, dark clouds, etc. Pull out each type of instrument to illustrate certain elements musically. Use a rainstick for "rain," thundertube for "dark clouds," tambourine for "sunshine," xylophone for "blue skies" and a scarf or streamer for "rainbow." If these specific elements are not suggested by the group, be prepared to suggest them yourself. Play part of the musical selection "I Can See Clearly Now" and instruct the group to listen specifically for the words "rain," "dark clouds," "sunshine," "blue skies" and "rainbow." Pass out the instruments and practice saying each of those words, with participants playing the correct corresponding instruments when their words are said. Listen to the musical selection again, instructing participants to only play their instrument when they hear the corresponding word sung on the recording.

Notes

♪ To simplify this activity, split the group in half and use only two musical/word cues.

75. Xylophone Conversation

Goal areas

- Communication skills: *Auditory perception, Expressive language, Initiating contact and communication*
- Social/emotional skills: *Teamwork, Impulse control*
- Leisure skills: *Imagination/creativity, Musical skill*

Materials

- Two xylophones with mallets

Activity

Have two participants at a time play xylophone duets. Either assign partners or have people take turns choosing partners (instruct that they must choose partners who haven't gone yet). Either person may initiate playing, but both must be verbally silent. They must listen to each other and have a conversation through the music only. Point out that they may want to listen and respond to each other's volume, tempo, style, etc., as part of the "conversation." When a pair has finished playing a duet together, elicit comments from the rest of the group about how the conversation seemed to have gone, or what it might have been about. Ask the participants to explain what they were "talking" about, and whether they adjusted their playing according to the other person's playing.

Notes

♪ Try assigning specific topics for the xylophone conversation.

♪ Be prepared to bring duets that run long to a close.

♪ You may choose to give participants one mallet or two, according to their physical and cognitive functioning levels.

76. Boomwhacker Beat

Goal areas

- Sensorimotor: *Gross motor, Sensory integration*
- Social/emotional skills: *Teamwork, Impulse control*
- Leisure skills: *Imagination/creativity, Musical skill*

Materials

- Three Boomwhackers in notes that create a major chord (e.g., C, E and G)

Activity

Demonstrate how to hit the Boomwhackers on the ground in a steady, metronomic fashion. Give two of the Boomwhackers to group members, and practice playing a steady pulse with all three Boomwhackers playing at once to create a repetitive chord. Create a steady beat and encourage the rest of the group to vocalize, hum, sing and create music within that chord structure. Repeat as many times as necessary, so that everyone who would like to play the Boomwhackers gets that chance.

Notes

♪ If group members seem to be struggling with vocally improvising on their own, you may choose to hum or sing a phrase that the rest of the group can then echo back.

♪ This activity may also be done with three-tone chimes or resonating bells. The overall effect will be different.

77. The Music Comes Over

Goal areas

- Cognitive skills: *Attention span*
- Sensorimotor: *Gross motor*
- Social/emotional skills: *Impulse control*

Materials

- Recorded music with a strong "walking" tempo beat, or guitar or piano
- Ample room to move in

Activity

Have participants line up on one side of the room. Play some music (live or recorded) and instruct the participants to walk to the other side of the room in time to the music. Stop the music at random points, instructing everyone to "freeze" when the music stops. If they keep moving or walk faster than the music, they must go back to start over. The first one across the room wins and can control the music, stopping and starting for another round, or can simply be cheered and congratulated for winning.

Notes

♪ Have an assistant push participants in wheelchairs across the room at a steady pace with the music. If possible, have the person in the wheelchair call out, "Stop!" to the assistant when they hear the music stop.

♪ If live music is used, you can vary the tempo, instructing the participants to adjust their walking speeds accordingly.

78. You Are

Goal areas

- Communication skills: *Expressive language*
- Cognitive skills: *Sequencing, Reality orientation*
- Social/emotional skills: *Identify/appropriately express emotion, Turn-taking*

Materials

- Guitar or piano
- Music for "You Are My Sunshine" by Oliver Hood
- Lyric sheet with blanks to fill in, dry-erase board or chalkboard
- Pencil, marker or chalk

Activity

Sing "You Are My Sunshine" then tell the group that they will take turns rewriting this song to someone special. Give each participant a turn to fill in the following blanks.

> "You are my _____, my only _____; you make me _____ when
> _____. You'll never know, dear, how much I love you. Please don't
> take my _____ away."

Notes

♪ Spend time processing feelings and discussing how each group member feels about the person they are singing about.

♪ For a similar, less involved activity to be used with lower-functioning or less-verbal participants, see Activity 8, "You Are My Sunshine."

79. Collective Mandala

Goal areas

- Academic skills: *Other*
- Cognitive skills: *Abstract thinking*
- Sensorimotor: *Fine motor, Sensory integration*
- Social/emotional skills: *Teamwork, Other*
- Leisure skills: *Imagination/creativity, Relaxation*

Materials

- A mandala that has been cut up into equal "pie-slice" pieces, with one section for each group member
- A copy of the mandala that has not been cut up, or a blank sheet of paper
- Colored pencils
- Glue or adhesive tape
- Recording of relaxing instrumental music
- A table to color on

Activity

Provide each group member with a section of the mandala and access to the colored pencils. Play the recording of relaxing instrumental music and ask the group to remain silent while listening to the music and coloring their mandala section, based on the colors that they imagine from the music or how the music makes them feel. Once everyone has finished, glue or tape the pieces together onto the uncut sheet of paper to make the mandala whole, and facilitate a discussion of how each person's section was different, but putting the sections together makes a unique, fascinating and beautiful whole picture.

Notes

♪ Choose a simple mandala design to keep the coloring aspect simple and to the activity short.

♪ Consider designing your own mandala, or find free printable mandalas on the Internet.

80. Turn, Turn, Turn

Goal areas

- Communication skills: *Expressive language*
- Academic skills: *Reading, Other*
- Cognitive skills: *Reality orientation, Memory*
- Sensorimotor: *Fine motor*
- Leisure skills: *Imagination/creativity*

Materials

- Guitar or keyboard
- Music for the song "Turn, Turn, Turn" by Peter Seeger, as recorded by The Byrds
- Dry-erase board
- Markers (preferably in a variety of colors) and eraser

Activity

Begin by singing the song "Turn, Turn, Turn" and inviting the group to sing along. Facilitate a discussion about what the song means and how there is a time and season for everything. Ask the group what the seasons of the year are and which season you are experiencing currently. Instruct the group to think of things that happen, or things you might see, in the current season (e.g., the fall season may include pumpkins, leaves, warm clothes, etc.). Give everyone a turn to come to the front and draw a picture on the dry-erase board of one thing they think of that happens or is seen during the season. Sing the song again, replacing the original lyrics with what has been drawn on the board.

Notes

♪ If appropriate to the group's cognitive and reading/writing skills, it may be more beneficial to have them write their suggestions instead of draw them. The result may also be a mix of written words and pictures, depending on what various group members are able or willing to do.

♪ Instead of things relevant to a season, this activity may be modified with group members by thinking of opposites (i.e., a time for "happiness, a time for "sadness) or periods or events in their lives.

81. Simple Songwriting

Goal areas

- Communication skills: *Expressive language*
- Cognitive skills: *Sequencing, Memory*
- Social/emotional skills: *Identify/appropriately express emotion, Teamwork*
- Leisure skills: *Imagination/creativity, Musical skill, Music appreciation*

Materials

- Large dry-erase board, chalkboard or an easel pad
- Markers or chalk
- Guitar or piano
- Assorted percussion instruments (optional)

Activity

Ask the group to pick a topic or theme for their song. Make suggestions if needed (e.g., a holiday or specific feelings). After a theme has been chosen, give each person the opportunity to think of a word or phrase that falls into the chosen category. Write these words down on the board so all group members can see them. After the words or short phrases have been collected, arrange them in a song format. Have the group choose what style they want their song to be written in (e.g., rock, country, dance). Use the guitar or piano to then play an appropriate chord progression to fit the song, based on the genre the group has chosen. Encourage the group to sing spontaneous melodies for the phrases in the song, initiating creativity by singing an example for the first words or phrase of the song. Reinforce both creativity and memory retention by repeating melodies that participants may come up with.

Notes

♪ Have any non-verbal group members choose a particular sound or instrument in place of a lyric. Feature that instrument or sound in the song. For example, wind chimes may be used to represent the winter wind in a Christmas song.

82. Musical Shapes

Goal areas

- Academic skills: *Other*
- Cognitive skills: *Sequencing, Analyzing, Memory*
- Sensorimotor: *Gross motor*

Materials

- Slow recorded music with strong meter feels of 4/4, 3/4 and 1.
- Scarves or rhythm sticks

Activity

Play one of the musical selections and ask the group to clap with the beat. See if anyone can anticipate where the strong beat is going to occur, and count out loud to reinforce the meter the music is in (e.g., "ONE, two, three," "ONE, two, three, four" or "ONE, ONE"). Pass out one scarf or rhythm stick to each person and demonstrate how the beats correspond to a shape by moving the scarf/stick through the air in time to the music: A count of three is a triangle, a count of four is a square and a count of one is a circle. Encourage everyone to copy the pattern. Repeat this with another musical selection, or two with different meters, until the group is comfortable with each meter and shape. Then randomly play each selection and see whether the participants can recall the shape to match each selection.

Notes

♪ Give clues to the group during random play by counting out loud.

83. Animal Adventure

Goal areas

- Communication skills: *Expressive language*
- Cognitive skills: *Sequencing, Abstract thinking, Memory, Attention span*
- Social/emotional skills: *Turn-taking, Teamwork*
- Leisure skills: *Imagination/creativity*

Materials

- Assorted percussion instruments with unique sounds, such as wind chimes, maracas, claves, shakers, triangles, rainsticks, ocean drums, slide whistles or triangles

Activity

Have the group sit in a circle with all of the instruments spread out in the center. Explain that you are going to write a story together, using music to bring it to life. Begin by asking the group to think of a special animal. Have the person who first volunteers an animal describe what that animal looks like, choose an instrument to represent this animal, and "play" this animal on the instrument. Say: "This animal is going to go on an adventure! Let's find out what it does!" Ask the next person in circle, "What is the first thing that this animal does in our story?" The next participant must then choose an instrument to represent her suggested action or idea. Continue around the circle, having each participant add another part to the story. Review the story regularly by going back to the beginning and having each person play their instrument, while you or they restate each part of the story. Finish with lavish praise for the wonderful story that they created as a group, and elicit one final performance of the story to tie it all together.

Notes

♪ If a client is non-verbal, encourage him to choose an instrument and play it, then ask other group members to suggest what it sounds like the animal in the story is doing.

♪ Be prepared to guide the final person in the group towards a story ending, or have the entire group improvise together and ask for suggestions on how the story should end based on what the music sounds like.

♪ You may choose to take written notes on the story as it unfolds. This can be the basis for future chapters during further group sessions.

♪ Instead of an animal, you may choose to start with a fictional person or fairy-tale character. Avoid using a known person, in order to avoid potential negative story parts that may be created.

♪ Create stories with other topics, such as a summer trip participants might like to take.

84. Do-Re-Mi Chimes

Goal areas

- Communication skills: *Auditory perception*
- Cognitive skills: *Sequencing, Memory, Attention span*
- Social/emotional skills: *Impulse control*
- Leisure skills: *Musical skill, Music appreciation*

Materials

- Guitar or piano
- Suzuki Tone Chimes (C major scale), or resonating bells (C major scale), with a mallet for each participant.
- Music for the song "Do-Re-Mi" from *The Sound of Music* by Rodgers/ Hammerstein

Activity

Sing the song "Do-Re-Mi" from the *Sound of Music* (Richard Rodgers/Oscar Hammerstein). Pass out a chime to each person, explaining and demonstrating how each note corresponds to a solfege syllable. Make sure each participant understands which solfege syllable they have in hand and practice singing that syllable while they play. Sing the song again with participants playing their chimes when the song gets to their solfege syllable. This activity can be repeated multiple times, increasing in tempo as it becomes more comfortable for the clients.

Notes

♪ To make this activity easier, hand out chimes in scale order, so that participants can see when they are going to be next.

♪ To make this activity more difficult, mix the chimes up. This encourages increased concentration and memory retention.

♪ Chimes/bells can be traded with someone else, and the song played and sung again.

85. Roll Your Fists Around

Goal areas

- Communication skills: *Receptive language*
- Cognitive skills: *Attention span*
- Sensorimotor: *Gross motor*

Materials

- Guitar or piano
- Music for "Roll Your Fists Around" by Kihoko Moriwaki (See Appendix A)

Activity

Sing the song "Roll Your Fists Around" while everyone makes fists with both hands and moves them in a circular rolling motion around each other in front of their chest, elbows bent. Follow the words in the song to place fists in various positions.

Notes

♪ Demonstrate the fist-rolling motion before beginning the activity. This motor skill may be difficult for many participants to grasp immediately.

86. Rhythm Shakers

Goal areas

- Communication skills: *Auditory perception*
- Sensorimotor: *Sensory integration*
- Social/emotional skills: *Teamwork, Impulse control*
- Leisure skills: *Musical skill*

Materials

- Egg shakers
- Maracas
- Jingle bell sticks
- Paddle drum (optional)

Activity

Split the group into two or three teams and designate each team to play a particular type of shaken instrument. Teach each team their own rhythm; have one team play quarter notes and another play eighth notes. A third team may play sixteenth notes by shaking back and forth (best done with egg shakers). Have the teams play together, encouraging everyone to keep playing their designated rhythm without being distracted by the other rhythms.

Notes

♪ Use a paddle or another drum to keep a steady beat and create a distinctive sound for the group to keep tempo with.

♪ Sing a familiar song a capella with the rhythms being played. This will help the group understand how the beats fit into music.

♪ Introduce the activity or make the activity easier by keeping a steady beat on the paddle drum and having the entire group play quarter, eighth or sixteenth notes all together.

87. Rhythmic Hot Potato

Goal areas

- Sensorimotor: *Gross motor*
- Social/emotional skills: *Turn-taking, Teamwork, Impulse control*

Materials

- Beanbags
- Recorded music with a strong 4/4 beat, or piano or drum

Activity

Start the music and draw attention to the beat, encouraging participants to feel the beat by clapping or patting their legs left and right. Have participants sit or stand in a circle with both hands out, palms up. Place a beanbag into one person's hand on the musical beat, and encourage the group members to pass the beanbag first from one hand to the next, then into their neighbor's open hand, all with the beat of the music, continuing around the circle. Emphasize use and discrimination of both hands by saying, "left, right, left, right" to indicate which hand to use and to emphasize connection with the musical beat.

Notes

♪ Demonstrate the beanbag-passing technique with each person individually when this activity is first introduced.

♪ Encourage everyone to place the beanbag into their neighbor's hand rather than tossing or dropping it.

♪ When a group is able to pass the beanbag around without direct physical facilitation, the facilitator may choose to play a drum or piano instead of a CD.

♪ Begin with slow music and increase speed according to participants' skill levels.

♪ As skills increase, introduce more beanbags into the circle.

88. Shake, Rattle and Roll

Goal areas

- Communication skills: *Auditory perception*
- Cognitive skills: *Sequencing, Attention span*
- Sensorimotor: *Sensory integration*
- Social/emotional skills: *Impulse control*

Materials

- Tambourines
- Shakers
- Paddle drums with mallets
- A recording of the song "Shake, Rattle and Roll" by Jesse Stone, as recorded by Bill Haley and His Comets

Activity

Pass out tambourines, shakers and paddle drums to the group. Demonstrate how the shakers "shake," the tambourines "rattle" and the paddle drums "roll." Practice calling out "shake," "rattle" or "roll," as participants with the corresponding instruments play them for each word called. Play the recorded music and encourage careful listening. Direct participants to play their instruments in the correct spots in the song. The rest of the song can be either all-play or nobody-play.

Notes

♪ To make the activity easier, group instrument types together. You can then direct each section more clearly.

♪ To increase difficulty for more highly cognitive groups, mix up the instruments and/or don't direct visually.

89. Film Scoring

Goal areas

- Communication skills: *Expressive language*
- Cognitive skills: *Sequencing, Abstract thinking, Memory*
- Social/emotional skills: *Identify/appropriately express emotion, Teamwork*
- Leisure skills: *Imagination/creativity, Music appreciation*

Materials

- TV with DVD player or VCR with remote
- DVD/s or VHS tape/s with two or more movie scenes that depict particular emotions (e.g., humor, suspense, happiness, love, excitement). At least one of these movie scenes should include a musical soundtrack
- Assorted musical instruments

Activity

Discuss the importance of music in film by asking questions such as whether participants' favorite movies have music that sounds exciting, sad or scary. Show a chosen movie scene silently, then with sound. Finally, play the sound without the picture. Discuss the differences. Then show a new movie scene without a soundtrack. Facilitate a discussion and experimentation time for the group to come up with a musical soundtrack appropriate for the movie scene, using available instruments. Play the scene again with the group's live musical soundtrack and discuss how their music enhanced the scene.

Notes

♪ Choose films that are age appropriate and have multiple characters.

90. Musical Charades

Goal areas

- Cognitive skills: *Abstract thinking, Analyzing*
- Sensorimotor: *Sensory integration*
- Leisure skills: *Imagination/creativity*

Materials

- Slips of paper with simple, familiar activities written on them that will be easy to act out (e.g., sleeping, eating, running, walking, getting dressed, talking with a friend, etc.)
- Bowl to draw the slips of paper from
- Assortment of percussion instruments

Activity

Ask each participant to take a turn pulling a slip of paper from the bowl. They must read them silently (assisted as needed) and each choose an instrument or two to use in acting out this activity. The rest of the group must then guess what the activity is.

Notes

♪ Make the activity easier by reading each slip of paper before putting it into the bowl, so that the group will have a hint at what to expect.

♪ Alternatively, you may provide blank slips of paper and ask for activity suggestions from the group to write on them.

♪ Make this activity more complex and teamwork oriented by writing scenarios for two to three participants to act out together.

91. Collaborative Drawing

Goal areas

- Communication skills: *Auditory perception, Expressive language*
- Academic skills: *Other*
- Cognitive skills: *Abstract thinking*
- Sensorimotor: *Fine motor, Sensory integration*
- Social/emotional skills: *Teamwork, Impulse control*
- Leisure skills: *Imagination/creativity, Relaxation*

Materials

- Large piece of butcher paper or other paper
- Colored pencils, crayons, oil pastels or other drawing mediums
- Table around which participants can gather comfortably
- Recording of relaxing instrumental music

Activity

Put the relaxing music on and instruct the group to imagine a peaceful place. Suggest a beach, meadow or similar location, if a suggestion isn't quickly made by the group . Place the paper on the center of the table and make a very basic outline of the place, if appropriate (e.g., a shoreline designating the beach and the water). Have participants continue to listen to the music and look at the paper, quietly imagining that place and what they might see there. Instruct the participants to pick up the drawing elements and add what they imagine is in that place. Examples may include plants, animals, favorite items, etc. Emphasize the fact that this is a group project, and everyone is allowed to add what they feel should be in the picture without reproach or negative comments from other participants. Once the picture is finished, facilitate a discussion about the various elements in the picture and how they are important to the participants.

Notes

♪ You may choose to use recorded music which includes nature sounds (e.g., ocean waves, birds chirping, rain), and ask the group what those sounds seem to be coming from, using the resulting imagery to choose the relaxing place that will be drawn.

♪ The finished picture may be used later as a focal point for musical improvisation.

92. Color to the Instruments

Goal areas

- Communication skills: *Auditory perception*
- Cognitive skills: *Memory, Attention span*
- Sensorimotor: *Fine motor, Sensory integration*

Materials

- Three small percussion instruments with distinct sounds (e.g., tambourine, shaker and triangle)
- Paper (blank or with simple shapes printed on it) for each participant
- A set of three specific colors in colored pencils or crayons for each participant
- Colored stickers or other identifying markers which match the pencil/crayon colors
- Pictures or drawing of the provided instruments which can be displayed for everyone to see
- A table for participants to draw/color on

Activity

Give each group member a sheet of paper and a set of three specific colored pencils or crayons (e.g., each person will get one red, one green and one blue). Have the group choose together which color will represent which instrument, and place the pictures of the three instruments where they can be seen. Place colored stickers to identify which colors correspond to which instruments. Begin playing one instrument at a time, switching randomly. Participants must pick up and use the correct matching color, switching when they hear the instrument change.

Notes

♪ Simplify or shorten the activity by specifying the colors associated with each instrument, rather than making it a choice.

♪ Increase or decrease the number of instruments/colors, depending on the participants' functioning levels, time allotted and size of the group.

♪ Increase difficulty or implement another learning element by having the group color in specific shapes (triangle, square, circle) according to which instrument is played.

♪ Increase difficulty by hiding the instruments while they are being played, to encourage the group to rely on auditory cues alone.

93. Musical Board Game

Goal areas

- Communication skills: *Receptive language*
- Academic skills: *Counting/Math, Reading*
- Cognitive skills: *Sequencing*
- Social/emotional skills: *Turn-taking, Other*

Materials

- One or two game dice
- Guitar or piano
- Small objects to be used as playing pieces
- Any instruments referred to in the game (see below)
- Piece of cardstock paper or poster board prepared ahead of time as follows: Draw horizontal lines on the paper to indicate 10–20 spaces from top to bottom. Write "Start" in the bottom space and "Finish" in the top space. Write various creative instructions in the rest of the spaces, such as:
  - Play 15 beats on the drum
  - Sing "You Are My Sunshine"
  - Tell us what your favorite food is
  - Sing your favorite song
  - Play a quick duet with another group member

Activity

Introduce the game to the group and explain the rules. The participants will take turns rolling the dice and can move their game piece forward the corresponding number of spaces. They must then follow the instructions written in that space. Their turn is then over. The first person to reach the finish line wins!

Notes

♪ Using one dice will make things go easier and more quickly.

♪ If time and circumstances permit, ask group members for suggestions on what to write in the empty spaces on the game board. Be creative!

94. Guitar Strum

Goal areas

- Sensorimotor: *Gross motor, Fine motor, Sensory integration*
- Social/emotional skills: *Turn-taking, Self-esteem*
- Leisure skills: *Musical skill*

Materials

- Acoustic guitar/s tuned to "open D" (strings tuned to D, A, D, F#, A, D)
- Pick/s, including adaptive pick if necessary
- Adaptive guitar slide/s (optional)
- Colored stickers placed on specific frets to signify the chords used in a simple, pre-planned, two- or three-chord song (optional)

Activity

This activity can be done as a group with multiple participants playing together if multiple guitars are available; or participants can take turns with the guitar, as the rest of the group is encouraged to participate through singing and watching. Demonstrate and practice holding the guitar (strap recommended). Help the group to experiment starting, stopping, playing loud and soft, fast and slow, etc., both individually and as a group.

Notes

♪ Encourage the participant and others in the group to sing freely while playing.

♪ For more advanced/higher-functioning players, an adaptive slide may be used to play different chords as the player moves the slide up the neck of the guitar. You may place color-coded stickers on different frets of the guitar to make it possible to play a two- or three-chord song. Only use this system when you are confident the players will be successful.

♪ For participants unable to hold or strum the guitar, hold the guitar yourself and encourage the participant to strum while you barre the chords.

95. Rhythm Pies

Goal areas

- Communication skills: *Auditory perception*
- Cognitive skills: *Sequencing*
- Sensorimotor: *Gross motor, Sensory integration*
- Social/emotional skills: *Impulse control*
- Leisure skills: *Musical skill*

Materials

- Two rhythm sticks for each person

Activity

Pass out a set of rhythm sticks to all participants. Use the syllables in the names of fruit and fruit pies as speech/musical rhythm indicators. For example, "ap-ple pie" would create the rhythm of two eighth notes followed by a quarter note. Tap the rhythm while saying these familiar words to facilitate understanding and memory retention of the rhythms. Have participants echo the rhythm that is played and spoken by the facilitator, by both playing and speaking in rhythm.

Notes

♪ This activity is helpful when the group is preparing to learn musical skills.

♪ Some examples of syllables that can match up with eighth notes, quarter note, sixteenth notes and triplets include *apple pie, huckleberry, strawberry.*

♪ Initially encourage participants to say the words while tapping the rhythm, but gradually move the participants toward copying the rhythm without saying the words.

♪ Mix up rhythms/words in increasing difficulty, e.g., "pie, pie, apple pie."

96. Music Listening Game

Goal areas

- Communication skills: *Auditory perception*
- Academic skills: *Other*
- Cognitive skills: *Analyzing, Reality orientation, Memory*
- Social/emotional skills: *Teamwork*
- Leisure skills: *Musical skill, Music appreciation*

Materials

- Recordings of various classical music selections

Activity

Split the group into two teams and designate team captains. Play an excerpt of music and ask the teams to discuss the music amongst themselves, with the team captains raising their hands when they have decided on certain facts about the music. Give points for identifying correct information regarding the excerpt, including instruments being played, composer's name, title of the piece, time period when the music was written, etc. These identifying facts may either be given spontaneously or be solicited with specifically questions, such as, "What instruments do you hear?"

Notes

♪ Visual references including pictures of instruments or real instruments may be helpful.

♪ This activity is best incorporated with a group who has been learning music appreciation skills and has learned about instruments, composers, etc.

♪ Alternatively, you may choose a different musical genre with which group members are familiar.

97. Index Card Songwriting

Goal areas

- Communication skills: *Receptive language*
- Cognitive skills: *Sequencing*
- Social/emotional skills: *Teamwork*
- Leisure skills: *Music appreciation*

Materials

- Piano
- Dry-erase board, chalkboard or easel pad
- Minimum of 12 index cards with rhythms printed or drawn on them: quarter note, half note, whole note or a pair of eighth notes
- Tape to stick the index cards on the board

Activity

Have participants take turns choosing 12 numbers between one and eight. Write these numbers and their corresponding musical pitches on the board (1=C, 2=D, 3=E, 4=F, 5=G, 6=A, 7=B, 8=C). Make sure these are widely spaced on the board. Have participants then take turns choosing an index card with a rhythm to place under each of the 12 numbers/notes. Play the resulting composition on the piano and discuss what feeling or thought the melody that has been created might express.

Notes

♪ A second half to this activity may involve the group creating lyrics to go with the melody they have composed.

98. Chordal Songwriting

Goal areas

- Communication skills: *Auditory perception*
- Cognitive skills: *Sequencing, Analyzing*
- Social/emotional skills: *Teamwork*
- Leisure skills: *Imagination/creativity, Musical skill, Music appreciation*

Materials

- Piano
- Dry-erase board, chalkboard or easel with paper pad
- Markers, chalk, pen

Activity

Before beginning the activity, write possible melody note names C, D, E, F, G, A, B on the board. Below these, write (in stacked columns) triad chords that can be used in the key of C (C/E/G; E/G/B; F/A/C, etc.). Ask group members to choose and circle three chords. Play the chords on the piano. Elicit feedback on whether the group likes the three chord pattern or whether they would like to change any of the chords. Then ask group members to choose two to four melody notes per chord. Play the melody notes and chords together on the piano and elicit feedback about what the group likes or does not like about the result. Adjust accordingly and encourage full group participation in changing their song until it sounds the way they would like.

Notes

♪ This can be a great opportunity for group members to practice working together as a team, compromising and giving/receiving feedback. Be prepared to redirect as needed according to group members' social skill levels.

99. Xylophone Ensemble

Goal areas

- Cognitive skills: *Sequencing, Attention span*
- Sensorimotor: *Sensory integration*
- Social/emotional skills: *Teamwork*
- Leisure skills: *Musical skill*

Materials

- Xylophone for each person
- Mallets for each person
- Colored stickers
- Poster board or paper with a simple song melody written out and represented by specific colors for each note

Activity

Before the activity, remove keys from the xylophones that are not used in the chosen song. Place colored stickers on the remaining keys with specific color coding matching the song chart. For example, put a red sticker on C, green on G, etc. Begin the activity by having each person identify the colors while playing each note on their xylophone. Introduce the poster with the song, after note/color correlation is grasped. Have the group play the notes with the colors that are pointed to by the facilitator, in order to play the song together.

Notes

♪ For increased cognitive difficulty and attention span, each person may instead be given a xylophone with notes/colors that are different from the other group members, each person then only playing their xylophone when "their" notes are pointed to.

♪ This activity may also be facilitated using tone chimes, resonating bells or hand bells.

100. Creative Sing-a-longs

Goal areas

- Communication skills: *Expressive language*
- Cognitive skills: *Abstract thinking, Analyzing, Reality orientation*
- Leisure skills: *Imagination/creativity, Musical skill, Music appreciation*

Materials

- Guitar, piano or recordings, if live accompaniment is not available
- Various percussion instruments

Activity

The standard group sing-a-long can be enhanced in many creative ways to address various areas of development:

- "Name That Tune," with the winner being allowed to play a tall drum or other distinctive instrument for the duration of the song.
- "Name That Tune" using recordings, with the winner being allowed to sing the song karaoke-style into a microphone with the recording.
- Play only the chords to a song and encourage participants to guess what the song is. Add a hint by humming the tune along with the chords.
- Have each group member play a different instrument along with the song. When the song ends, everyone passes their instrument to the right or left, playing a new instrument with each song.
- Use contrasting styles of recorded music (e.g., pop, country, Latin, etc.) and discuss how the styles are different and which ones the participants prefer.
- Sing a song related in some way to a well-known holiday; ask the group to guess what holiday it might be and recall other songs related to that holiday.
- Facilitate a short discussion after each song about what the composer might have been thinking or feeling while writing the song.

Notes

♪ Don't underestimate the power of a sing-a-long to redirect focus, encourage participation and enhance social interaction! Be creative with it to keep it fresh and interesting both for the group and for yourself.

Appendix A: Sheet Music
for Original Songs

Smile and Wave

Minako Kamimura

I Like to Sing

Minako Kamimura

Let's All Play Together

Kelly Summer

Let's   all   play to-ge - ther   as   a   group.____
Drum____   plays_____   by   its - self._____
Every - body play to-ge - ther   as   a   group.____

Let's   all   play to-ge - ther__   as   a   group.   Can we
Drum____   plays_____   by   its - self.   Can she
Every - body play   to-ge - ther____   as   a   group.   Can we

play it?__   Can   we   play it?__   Can we   play it?___
play it?__   Can   she play it?__   Can she play it?___
play it?__   Can   we   play it?__   We   can play it!_____

Optional vamp meaures.
6-9 on final repeat

Eve - ry - bo - dy   stop!
All   to - ge - ther   now!

I'm in the Mood

Minako Kamimura

The Weekend Song

Maria Ramey

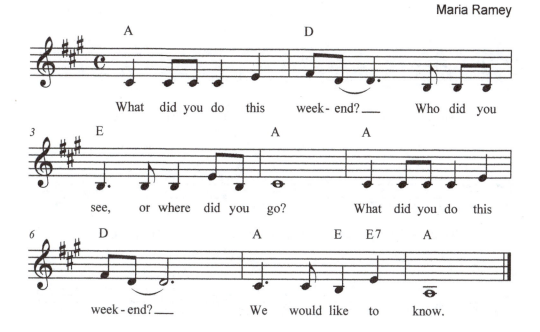

Clap Your Hands, One Two Three

Minako Kamimura

Clap your hands Sar - ah, One, Two, Three.

Clap your hands Sar - ah, One, Two, Three. You and me -

clap - ping ha - nds. One, Two, Three.

Just for Fun

Maria Ramey

Oh his name is John - ny, yes it is. And he

watch-es T - V __ just for fun. Oh his name is John - ny and he

watch-es T - V, yes he watch-es it 'til he is done.

Howl at the Moon

Kelly Summer

Cha, Cha, Cha

Kihoko Moriwaki

Colors Everywhere

Maria Ramey

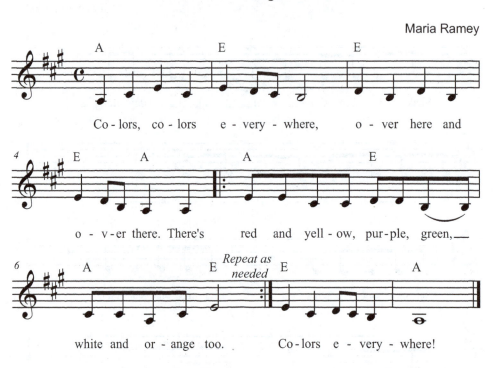

Co-lors, co-lors e-very-where, o-ver here and

o-v-er there. There's red and yell-ow, pur-ple, green,

white and or-ange too. Co-lors e-very-where!

Wave the Scarves

Kihoko Moriwaki

Clap Your Hands to the Music

Kihoko Moriwaki

Move to the Music

Kihoko Moriwaki

Who's in the Marching Band?

Lindsay Felchle

Roll Your Fists Around

Kihoko Moriwaki

Appendix B:
List of Books Illustrating
Well-Known Songs

These books may be found new or used at a variety of online or brick-and-mortar bookstores, online auction sites or in your local library. Many of these books include a CD recording of the song. This is only a sampling of the many books available which illustrate well-known songs.

America the Beautiful
by Katharine Bates. Illustrated by Wendell Minor.
New York: Penguin Group. (2003)

My Favorite Things
by Richard Rodgers and Oscar Hammerstein. Illustrated by Renee Graef.
New York: HarperCollins Publishers. (2001)

Over the Rainbow
Composed by Harold Arlen. Performed by Judy Collins. Illustrated by Eric Puybaret.
Watertown, MA: Charlesbridge Publishing, Inc. (2010)

Sunshine on My Shoulders
by John Denver. Illustrated by Christopher Canyon.
Nevada City, CA: Dawn Publications. (2003)

Take Me Home, Country Roads
by John Denver. Adapted and illustrated by Christopher Canyon.
Nevada City, CA: Dawn Publications. (2005)

Puff, the Magic Dragon
by Peter Yarrow and Lenny Lipton. Illustrated by Eric Puybaret.
New York: Sterling Publishing. (2007)

This Land Is Your Land
by Woody Guthrie. Illustrated by Kathy Jakobsen.
Boston, MA: Little, Brown Books for Young Readers. (2008)

What a Wonderful World
by George David Weiss and Bob Thiele. Illustrated by Ashley Bryan.
New York: Simon & Schuster Children's Publishing. (1995)

Appendix C: List of Songs Referred to in Activities

An asterisk (*) indicates an original song by a contributor. These songs are included in this book with both melody and chord notations, and are provided on the enclosed CD. Corresponding activity numbers are in parentheses.

"Baby Elephant Walk" by Henry Mancini, 1961 (36)

"B-I-N-G-O" Traditional folk song (67)

"Boom Boom, Ain't it Great to Be Crazy" Traditional folk song (68)

* "Cha, Cha, Cha" by Kihoko Moriwaki, 2005 (44)

* "Clap Your Hands, One Two Three" by Minako Kamimura, 2001 (21)

* "Clap Your Hands to the Music" by Kihoko Moriwaki, 2005 (55)

* "Colors Everywhere" by Maria Ramey, 2007 (49)

"Do-Re-Mi" by Richard Rodgers and Oscar Hammerstein, 1959; as sung by Julie Andrews in *The Sound of Music*, 1965 (84)

"Do Wah Diddy Diddy" by Jeff Barry and Ellie Greenwich, 1963; as recorded by Manfred Mann, 1964 (35)

"The Hokey Pokey" Traditional folk song (30)

"Hot, Hot, Hot" by Alphonsus Cassell, 1982 (36)

* "Howl at the Moon" by Kelly Summer, 2009 (26)

"I Can See Clearly Now" by Johnny Nash, 1972 (74)

"I Feel Good" by James Brown, 1965 (22)

"If You're Happy and You Know It" Traditional Latvian folk song (12)

* "I'm in the Mood" by Minako Kamimura, 2001 (6)

"I've Been Working on the Railroad" Traditional American folk song (10)

* "I Like to Sing" by Minako Kamimura, 2001 (3)

"I Love the Mountains" Traditional folk song (19)

"I Won't Back Down" by Tom Petty, 1989 (69)

* "Just for Fun" by Maria Ramey, 2010 (24)

"La Raspa" Traditional Mexican folk song (48)

* "Let's All Play Together" by Kelly Summer, 2009 (4)

"Locomotion" by Gerry Goffin and Carole King, 1962 (36)

"Manic Monday" by Prince, 1984; as recorded by The Bangles, 1986 (46)

* "Move to the Music" by Kihoko Moriwaki, 2005 (56)

"My Favorite Things" by Richard Rodgers and Oscar Hammerstein, 1959; as sung by Julie Andrews in *The Sound of Music*, 1965. (43)

"Old MacDonald" Traditional folk song (20)

"Olympic Fanfare and Theme" by John Williams, 1984 (36)

"Over the Rainbow" by Harold Arlen and E.Y. Harburg, 1938 (18)

* "Roll Your Fists Around" by Kihoko Moriwaki, 2007 (85)

"Shake, Rattle and Roll" by Jesse Stone, 1954; as recorded by Bill Haley and His Comets, 1954 (88)

* "Smile and Wave" by Minako Kamimura, 2001 (2)

"Turn, Turn, Turn" by Peter Seeger, 1959; as recorded by The Byrds, 1965 (80)

"Twelve Days of Christmas" Traditional English Christmas carol (27)

"The Twist" by Hank Ballard, 1959; as recorded by Chubby Checker, 1960 (41)

* "Wave the Scarves" by Kihoko Moriwaki, 2005 (52)

* "The Weekend Song" by Maria Ramey, 2010 (7)

"When the Saints Go Marching In" by Virgil Stamps, 1937 (45) (58)

* "Who's in the Marching Band?" by Lindsay Felchle, 2010 (71)

"You Are My Sunshine" by Oliver Hood, 1939 (8) (78)

Appendix D: Supply Resources

This list is current as of the publishing date of this book. See www.group-music-activities.com for an updated list of suppliers.

Music in Motion
P.O. Box 869231
Plano, TX 75086
Tel: 800-807-3520
Fax: 972-943-8906
www.musicmotion.com

Music Is Elementary
5220 Mayfield Road
Cleveland, OH 44124
Tel: 800-888-7502
Fax: 440-461-3631
www.musiciselementary.com

Rhythm Band Instruments
P.O. Box 126
Fort Worth, Texas 76102
Tel: 800-424-4724
www.rhythmband.com

Suzuki Music
Education Division
P.O. Box 710459
Santee, CA 92072
Tel: 800-845-1594
Fax: 619-873-1997
www.suzukimusic.com/education

West Music
P.O. Box 5521
Coralville, IA 52241
Tel: 800-397-9378
Fax: 888-470-3942
www.westmusic.com

Appendix E: Contributors

Lindsay Felchle is a music therapist at Creative Identity, a non-profit fine arts program for adults with developmental disabilities in Anaheim, CA. She received her Bachelor of Arts degree in Music Therapy from California State University, Northridge.

Minako Kamimura is a music therapist at Hope University, a non-profit fine arts program for adults with developmental disabilities in Anaheim, CA. She received her Bachelor of Music degree in Music Therapy from Michigan State University.

Susie Kwon is a music therapist at Hope University, a non-profit fine arts program for adults with developmental disabilities in Anaheim, CA. She received a Bachelor of Science in Music and Associate of Science in Piano Pedagogy from Pacific Union College, a Music Therapy Equivalency degree from Chapman University and a Master's degree in Education, emphasis on community counseling, from Andrews University.

Kihoko Moriwaki is a music therapist at Hope University, a non-profit fine arts program for adults with developmental disabilities in Anaheim, CA. She received her Bachelor of Arts degree in Music Therapy from California State University, Northridge.

Vera Otsuka is a music therapist at Hope University, a non-profit fine arts program for adults with developmental disabilities in Anaheim, CA. She received her Bachelor of Music degree in Music Therapy from Berklee College of Music.

Maria Ramey is a music therapist at Hope University, a non-profit fine arts program for adults with developmental disabilities in Anaheim, CA, and at Royale Healthcare Therapeutic Residential Center, a psychiatric hospital in Santa Ana, CA. She received her Bachelor of Arts degree in Music Therapy from California State University, Northridge.

Kelly Summer is a music therapist in private practice with extensive experience working with adults with developmental disabilities in Long Beach, CA. She received a Bachelor of Music degree in Vocal Jazz Performance from University of Miami, a Master's degree in Vocal Jazz Performance from University of Southern California and received her Music Therapy equivalency degree from California State University, Northridge.

Appendix F: Activities Listed by Goal Area

Communication skills
Auditory perception

I Like to Sing (3)

Live Music Relaxation (11)

Matching Loud and Soft (23)

Paint the Air (25)

Random Duet (28)

Emotion Connection (29)

Concerto Soloist (31)

How Many Beats? (34)

Jump and Jive (39)

Follow My Beat (42)

Shake a Question (53)

Guess That Sound (54)

Musical Feelings (61)

Drum Q&A (64)

Marching Band (71)

I Can See Clearly Now (74)

Xylophone Conversation (75)

Do-Re-Mi Chimes (84)

Rhythm Shakers (86)

Shake, Rattle and Roll (88)

Collaborative Drawing (91)

Color to the Instruments (92)

Rhythm Pies (95)

Music Listening Game (96)

Chordal Songwriting (98)

Receptive language

Smile and Wave (2)

Let's All Play Together (4)

Shake up High (12)

Clap Your Hands, One Two Three (21)

Howl at the Moon (26)

Stretchy Band Hokey Pokey (30)

How Many Beats? (34)

Walk Like the Music (36)

Cha, Cha, Cha (44)

Wave the Scarves (52)

Shake a Question (53)

Clap Your Hands to the Music (55)

Move to the Music (56)

Marching In (58)

Leadership: African Drumming (70)

Marching Band (71)

I Can See Clearly Now (74)

Roll Your Fists Around (85)

Musical Board Game (93)

Index Card Songwriting (97)

Expressive language

I'm in the Mood (6)

The Weekend Song (7)

You Are My Sunshine (8)

Visual Lyric Analysis (13)

I Love… (19)

I Feel Good (22)

Howl at the Moon (26)

Emotion Connection (29)

Visual CDs (37)

My Favorite Things (43)

Signs of the Seasons (45)

Manic Monday (46)

News from Home (47)

This Is Me (51)

Musical Ball (60)

Musical Feelings (61)

Party Animal (62)

Celebration Song (63)

Your Story Through a Song (66)

I Won't Back Down (69)

What I Like About You (73)

Xylophone Conversation (75)

You Are (78)

Turn, Turn, Turn (80)

Simple Songwriting (81)

Animal Adventure (83)

Film Scoring (89)

Collaborative Drawing (91)

Creative Sing-a-longs (100)

Initiating contact and communication

Play the Tambourine (1)

The Weekend Song (7)

Triangle Teams (9)

Shaking to the Music Beat (10)

Just for Fun (24)

Mirroring (40)

News from Home (47)

Shake a Question (53)

Drum Q&A (64)

Leadership: African Drumming (70)

Eye Choose You (72)

Xylophone Conversation (75)

Academic skills

Counting/Math

Twelve Days (27)

How Many Beats? (34)

Song Bingo (59)

Musical Board Game (93)

Reading

Visual Lyric Analysis (13)

Musical Ball (60)

Rhythm Sticks Alphabet (65)

Five Letter Favorites (67)

Turn, Turn, Turn (80)

Musical Board Game (93)

Other

Paint the Air (25)

Twelve Days (27)

Stretchy Band Hokey Pokey (30)

Traveling Places (48)

Colors Everywhere (49)

Shake a Question (53)

Rhythm Sticks Alphabet (65)

Five Letter Favorites (67)

Collective Mandala (79)

Turn, Turn, Turn (80)

Musical Shapes (82)

Collaborative Drawing (91)

Music Listening Game (96)

Cognitive skills

Sequencing

Visual Lyric Analysis (13)

I Love… (19)

Twelve Days (27)

Conducting (32)

How Many Beats? (34)

Follow My Beat (42)

My Favorite Things (43)

Signs of the Seasons (45)

Manic Monday (46)

Wave the Scarves (52)

Song Bingo (59)

Five Letter Favorites (67)

Boom Boom (68)

I Can See Clearly Now (74)

You Are (78)

Simple Songwriting (81)

Musical Shapes (82)

Animal Adventure (83)

Do-Re-Mi Chimes (84)

Shake, Rattle and Roll (88)

Film Scoring (89)

Musical Board Game (93)

Rhythm Pies (95)

Index Card Songwriting (97)

Chordal Songwriting (98)

Xylophone Ensemble (99)

Abstract thinking

Frame Drum Imagination (16)

Over the Rainbow (18)

Paint the Air (25)

Conducting (32)

Guess the Hidden Instrument (33)

Visual CDs (37)

Traveling Places (48)

Dance Conducting (57)

Party Animal (62)

Celebration Song (63)

Rhythm Sticks Alphabet (65)

Five Letter Favorites (67)

Collective Mandala (79)

Animal Adventure (83)

Film Scoring (89)

Musical Charades (90)

Collaborative Drawing (91)

Creative Sing-a-longs (100)

Analyzing

You Are My Sunshine (8)

Paint the Air (25)

Guess the Hidden Instrument (33)

Visual CDs (37)

This Is Me (51)

Guess That Sound (54)

Musical Shapes (82)

Musical Charades (90)

Music Listening Game (96)

Chordal Songwriting (98)

Creative Sing-a-longs (100)

Reality orientation

The Weekend Song (7)

You Are My Sunshine (8)

I Feel Good (22)

Just for Fun (24)

My Favorite Things (43)

Signs of the Seasons (45)

Manic Monday (46)

News from Home (47)

Musical Ball (60)

Your Story Through a Song (66)

I Won't Back Down (69)

You Are (78)

Turn, Turn, Turn (80)

Music Listening Game (96)

Creative Sing-a-longs (100)

Memory

The Weekend Song (7)

Just for Fun (24)

Twelve Days (27)

How Many Beats? (34)

Follow My Beat (42)

My Favorite Things (43)

Manic Monday (46)

Guess That Sound (54)

Musical Ball (60)

Celebration Song (63)

Boom Boom (68)

Turn, Turn, Turn (80)

Simple Songwriting (81)

Musical Shapes (82)

Animal Adventure (83)

Do-Re-Mi Chimes (84)

Film Scoring (89)

Color to the Instruments (92)

Music Listening Game (96)

Attention span

Visual Lyric Analysis (13)

Old MacDonald Had a Band (20)

Matching Loud and Soft (23)

Concerto Soloist (31)

Conducting (32)

How Many Beats? (34)

Mirroring (40)

Follow My Beat (42)

Cha, Cha, Cha (44)

Colors Everywhere (49)

Wave the Scarves (52)

Clap Your Hands to the Music (55)

Move to the Music (56)

Song Bingo (59)

Boom Boom (68)

Eye Choose You (72)

I Can See Clearly Now (74)

The Music Comes Over (77)

Animal Adventure (83)

Do-Re-Mi Chimes (84)

Roll Your Fists Around (85)

Shake, Rattle and Roll (88)

Color to the Instruments (92)

Xylophone Ensemble (99)

Sensorimotor
Gross motor

Scarf Dance (5)

I'm in the Mood (6)

Triangle Teams (9)

Shake up High (12)

Over the Rainbow (18)

Clap Your Hands, One Two Three (21)

Paint the Air (25)

Howl at the Moon (26)

Random Duet (28)

Stretchy Band Hokey Pokey (30)

Walkin' Down the Street (35)

Walk Like the Music (36)

Jump and Jive (39)

Mirroring (40)

Twist (41)

Wave the Scarves (52)

Shake a Question (53)

Clap Your Hands to the Music (55)

Move to the Music (56)

Dance Conducting (57)

Marching In (58)

Musical Ball (60)

Marching Band (71)

Boomwhacker Beat (76)

The Music Comes Over (77)

Musical Shapes (82)

Roll Your Fists Around (85)

Rhythmic Hot Potato (87)

Guitar Strum (94)

Rhythm Pies (95)

Fine motor

Triangle Teams (9)

Shake up High (12)

Twist (41)

Song Bingo (59)

Collective Mandala (79)

Turn, Turn, Turn (80)

Collaborative Drawing (91)

Color to the Instruments (92)

Guitar Strum (94)

Sensory integration

Scarf Dance (5)

Over the Rainbow (18)

Old MacDonald Had a Band (20)

Clap Your Hands, One Two Three (21)

Paint the Air (25)

Random Duet (28)

Stretchy Band Hokey Pokey (30)

Guess the Hidden Instrument (33)

Walkin' Down the Street (35)

Jump and Jive (39)

Follow My Beat (42)

Nature Box (50)

Wave the Scarves (52)

Shake a Question (53)

Clap Your Hands to the Music (55)

Move to the Music (56)

Dance Conducting (57)

Song Bingo (59)

Musical Ball (60)

Marching Band (71)

Boomwhacker Beat (76)

Collective Mandala (79)

Rhythm Shakers (86)

Shake, Rattle and Roll (88)

Musical Charades (90)

Collaborative Drawing (91)

Color to the Instruments (92)

Guitar Strum (94)

Rhythm Pies (95)

Xylophone Ensemble (99)

Social/emotional skills

Identify/appropriately express emotion

Smile and Wave (2)

Let's All Play Together (4)

You Are My Sunshine (8)

I Feel Good (22)

Emotion Connection (29)

Visual CDs (37)

Pick a Card: Feelings (38)

My Favorite Things (43)

News from Home (47)

Musical Feelings (61)

Celebration Song (63)

I Won't Back Down (69)

You Are (78)

Simple Songwriting (81)

Film Scoring (89)

Turn-taking

Play the Tambourine (1)

Pick a Card: Instruments (15)

I Feel Good (22)

Just for Fun (24)

Howl at the Moon (26)

Twelve Days (27)

Concerto Soloist (31)

Conducting (32)

How Many Beats? (34)

Walkin' Down the Street (35)

Visual CDs (37)

Pick a Card: Feelings (38)

Mirroring (40)

Twist (41)

Follow My Beat (42)

News from Home (47)

Marching In (58)

Drum Q&A (64)

Your Story Through a Song (66)

Boom Boom (68)

Leadership: African Drumming (70)

Marching Band (71)

You Are (78)

Animal Adventure (83)

Rhythmic Hot Potato (87)

Musical Board Game (93)

Guitar Strum (94)

Teamwork

Triangle Teams (9)

Cluster Drumming (14)

Howl at the Moon (26)

Stretchy Band Hokey Pokey (30)

Concerto Soloist (31)

Conducting (32)

Walkin' Down the Street (35)

Dance Conducting (57)

Leadership: African Drumming (70)

Marching Band (71)

Xylophone Conversation (75)

Boomwhacker Beat (76)

Collective Mandala (79)

Simple Songwriting (81)

Animal Adventure (83)

Rhythm Shakers (86)

Rhythmic Hot Potato (87)

Film Scoring (89)

Collaborative Drawing (91)

Music Listening Game (96)

Index Card Songwriting (97)

Chordal Songwriting (98)

Xylophone Ensemble (99)

Impulse control

Cluster Drumming (14)

Old MacDonald Had a Band (20)

Matching Loud and Soft (23)

Random Duet (28)

Concerto Soloist (31)

How Many Beats? (34)

Mirroring (40)

Cha, Cha, Cha (44)

Move to the Music (56)

Dance Conducting (57)

Musical Ball (60)

Boom Boom (68)

I Can See Clearly Now (74)

Xylophone Conversation (75)

Boomwhacker Beat (76)

The Music Comes Over (77)

Do-Re-Mi Chimes (84)

Rhythm Shakers (86)

Rhythmic Hot Potato (87)

Shake, Rattle and Roll (88)

Collaborative Drawing (91)

Rhythm Pies (95)

Self-esteem

This Is Me (51)

Boom Boom (68)

What I Like About You (73)

Guitar Strum (94)

Other

Play the Tambourine (1)

Shaking to the Music Beat (10)

Just for Fun (24)

Shake a Question (53)

Guess That Sound (54)

Party Animal (62)

Eye Choose You (72)

Collective Mandala (79)

Musical Board Game (93)

Leisure skills

Imagination/creativity

Scarf Dance (5)

I'm in the Mood (6)

Shake up High (12)

Cluster Drumming (14)

Frame Drum Imagination (16)

Over the Rainbow (18)

I Love... (19)

I Feel Good (22)

Paint the Air (25)

Stretchy Band Hokey Pokey (30)

Concerto Soloist (31)

Walkin' Down the Street (35)

Visual CDs (37)

Mirroring (40)

Twist (41)

Traveling Places (48)

Nature Box (50)

Dance Conducting (57)

Marching In (58)

Party Animal (62)

Celebration Song (63)

Boom Boom (68)

Leadership: African Drumming (70)

What I Like About You (73)

Xylophone Conversation (75)

Boomwhacker Beat (76)

Collective Mandala (79)

Turn, Turn, Turn (80)

Simple Songwriting (81)

Animal Adventure (83)

Film Scoring (89)

Musical Charades (90)

Collaborative Drawing (91)

Chordal Songwriting (98)

Creative Sing-a-longs (100)

Musical skill

I Like to Sing (3)

Cluster Drumming (14)

Concerto Soloist (31)

Follow My Beat (42)

Guess That Sound (54)

Leadership: African Drumming (70)

Marching Band (71)

Xylophone Conversation (75)

Boomwhacker Beat (76)

Simple Songwriting (81)

Do-Re-Mi Chimes (84)

Rhythm Shakers (86)

Guitar Strum (94)

Rhythm Pies (95)

Music Listening Game (96)

Chordal Songwriting (98)

Xylophone Ensemble (99)

Creative Sing-a-longs (100)

Music appreciation

Visual Lyric Analysis (13)

Over the Rainbow (18)

I Love… (19)

Conducting (32)

Visual CDs (37)

Song Bingo (59)

Your Story Through a Song (66)

Leadership: African Drumming (70)

Simple Songwriting (81)

Do-Re-Mi Chimes (84)

Film Scoring (89)

Music Listening Game (96)

Index Card Songwriting (97)

Chordal Songwriting (98)

Creative Sing-a-longs (100)

Relaxation

Live Music Relaxation (11)

Heartbeat (17)

Paint the Air (25)

Nature Box (50)

Collective Mandala (79)

Collaborative Drawing (91)

Appendix G: CD Track Listing

1. "Smile and Wave" by Minako Kamimura
2. "I Like to Sing" by Minako Kamimura
3. "Let's All Play Together" by Kelly Summer
4. "I'm in the Mood" by Minako Kamimura
5. "The Weekend Song" by Maria Ramey
6. "Clap Your Hands, One Two Three" by Minako Kamimura
7. "Just for Fun" by Maria Ramey
8. "Howl at the Moon" by Kelly Summer
9. "Cha, Cha, Cha" by Kihoko Moriwaki
10. "Colors Everywhere": by Maria Ramey
11. "Wave the Scarves" by Kihoko Moriwaki
12. "Clap Your Hands to the Music" by Kihoko Moriwaki
13. "Move to the Music" by Kihoko Moriwaki
14. "Who's in the Marching Band?" by Lindsay Felchle
15. "Roll Your Fists Around" by Kihoko Moriwaki
16. Instrument Sound: Shaker
17. Instrument Sound: Tambourine
18. Instrument Sound: Paddle drum
19. Instrument Sound: Maracas
20. Instrument Sound: Ocean drum
21. Instrument Sound: Cabasa
22. Instrument Sound: Claves
23. Instrument Sound: Rainstick
24. Instrument Sound: Xylophone
25. Instrument Sound: Bar chimes
26. Instrument Sound: Bells
27. Instrument Sound: Boomwhackers

References

Boxill, E. (1985) *Music Therapy for the Developmentally Disabled.* Austin, TX: Pro-Ed.

Braddock, D., Hemp, R. and Rizzolo, M. (2008) *The State of the States in Developmental Disabilities.* Boulder, CO: Department of Psychiatry and Coleman Institute for Cognitive Disabilities, The University of Colorado.

Meyers, J. (2008) *How to Teach Daily Living Skills to Adults with Developmental Disabilities.* New York: iUniverse.

Nordoff Robbins Center for Music Therapy (2007) *History.* Available at http://steinhardt.nyu.edu/music/nordoff/history, accessed on November 7, 2010.

Schalkwijk, F. (2000) *Music and People with Developmental Disabilities* (2nd edition). London: Jessica Kingsley Publishers.

Activities for Adults with Learning Disabilities

Having Fun, Meeting Needs

Helen Sonnet and Ann Taylor

ISBN 9781843109754

Paperback: £17.99/$29.95

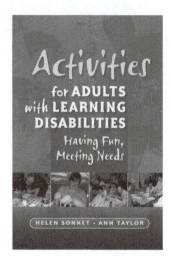

"This book is a fantastic resource, one which has truly inspired and helped us to become more creative when devising activities for adults with learning disabilities and has our full recommendation."

—PMLD Journal

This valuable resource for people working with adults with learning disabilities provides over 60 sessions of fun and engaging activities that aim to entertain and stimulate the minds of people with learning disabilities.

The sessions are divided into different types of activity including cookery, arts and crafts, drama and dance, and outside events. A comprehensive collection of varied and enjoyable activities, this practical book also contains useful tips to ensure that sessions run smoothly. All the activities are tried and tested by experienced practitioners and include a key advising the level of help required, wheelchair user suitability and any related health and safety issues involved.

Ideal for use in social clubs or residential homes, this is an essential toolkit for professionals and volunteers working with adults with learning disabilities.

Helen Sonnet is a teacher and author with over 30 years' experience in education. Helen specializes in working with children with learning and behavioral difficulties and does voluntary work at a Gateway Club for adults and children with learning disabilities. She lives in Somerset, UK. **Ann Taylor** trained as a teacher and has 30 years of experience working with adults with learning disabilities. Ann has been a Gateway Club leader for 12 years. She also lives in Somerset, UK.

Promoting Social Interaction for Individuals with Communicative Impairments

Making Contact

Edited by M. Suzanne Zeedyk

ISBN 9781843105398

Paperback: £17.99/$29.95

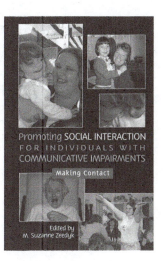

All humans have an innate need and ability to communicate with others, and this book presents successful approaches to nurturing communicative abilities in people who have some type of communication impairment.

The contributors look at a wide range of approaches, including Intensive Interaction, co-creative communication, sensory integration and music therapy, for a variety of impairments, including autism, profound learning disabilities, deafblindness, severe early neglect and dementia. This wide perspective provides insight into what it feels like to struggle with a communicative impairment, and how those who work with and care about such individuals can and should think more creatively about how to make contact with them.

Covering both the theory and practical implementation of different interventions, this book will be invaluable for health and social work professionals, psychologists, psychotherapists, counselors, and speech and language therapists, as well as researchers, teachers and students in these fields.

M. Suzanne Zeedyk, Ph.D., M.Phil., is Senior Lecturer in Developmental Psychology at the University of Dundee, UK. She has published a number of research articles on imitation and parent–child interaction, as well as other areas of psychology. The contributors to this volume comprise a range of researchers and practitioners experienced in working with individuals with communicative impairments. As well as being specialists in their individual domains, this set of authors have spent time working together as a group and thus are able to draw out often unrecognized connections between these domains.

Using Intensive Interaction with a Person with a Social or Communicative Impairment

Graham Firth and Mark Barber
ISBN 9781849051095
Paperback: £12.99/$21.95

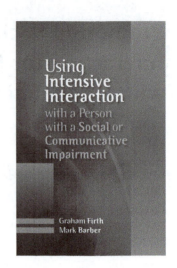

"It is clear that the writers have a deep knowledge and commitment to Intensive Interaction and these qualities underpin the worth of the book. This book is of value to those considering using Intensive Interaction in their work with people with profound and complex intellectual disability and as such may be considered a useful introduction to the subject."

—*The Frontline of Learning Disability Journal*

Intensive Interaction is a highly effective approach for communicating and developing social interaction and engagement with difficult-to-reach individuals. This easy-to-use guide steers readers through the practical application of the approach, showing how positive results can best be achieved.

The authors explain clearly how to prepare for, carry out and reflect on the use of Intensive Interaction with a client or family member. A multitude of key questions are addressed, including finding the right setting, evaluating progress and disengaging effectively at the end of a session. In the final section they consider some of the wider implications of the approach, such as developing confidence as a practitioner and incorporating Intensive Interaction into long-term care or educational planning.

This practical and accessible book is a useful resource for speech and language therapists, occupational therapists, special school or further education teachers, social care professionals and anyone else caring for or working with people with social or communicative impairments. It will also be useful to practitioners already using the approach.

Graham Firth is the current Intensive Interaction Project Leader for the Leeds Partnerships NHS Trust, UK. He was previously a further education teacher for adults with severe or profound learning disabilities. **Mark Barber** coordinates Intensive Interaction at Bayside Special Developmental School in Melbourne, Australia. He also works as a Consultant in Profound Intellectual Disability and Severe Communication Impairment in Australia and New Zealand.

Pied Piper

Musical Activities to Develop Basic Skills

John Bean and Amelia Oldfield

ISBN 9781853029943

Paperback: £16.99/$26.95

It is widely acknowledged that music is of great value for people with learning difficulties. It can be used as a catalyst to help those with special needs to acquire and improve basic skills and thereby to communicate better. With clear aims and easy-to-follow instructions, *Pied Piper* describes 78 enjoyable music activities for groups of children or adults who may have learning difficulties. The emphasis is on using music, rather than learning songs or rhythms, so group members do not need any special skills to be able to participate. Full details are given about any equipment required for the games, as well as suggestions for variations or modifications.

Designed to encourage people to develop their own ideas and musical activities, this collection will be a source of inspiration and practical advice for anyone, including carers and group leaders, working with people with a range of special needs.

John Bean studied the cello at the Royal Academy of Music and completed his music therapy training at the Guildhall School of Music and Drama, UK. For 12 years he held the position of senior music therapist for Leicestershire Education Authority. He has also worked as a professional cellist in symphony orchestras, chamber music groups and as a cello teacher. He now employs these skills in freelance work. **Amelia Oldfield** is a well-known and prestigious music therapist with over 25 years' experience in the field. She works at the Croft Unit for Child and Family Psychiatry and she lectures at Anglia Ruskin University, where she co-initiated the MA in Music Therapy Training. She is married with four children and plays clarinet in local chamber music groups in Cambridge, UK.

Let's All Listen

Songs for Group Work in Settings that Include Students with Learning Difficulties and Autism

Pat Lloyd

Foreword by Adam Ockelford

ISBN 9781843105831

Paperback: £24.99/$39.95

"I thoroughly recommend this title. You don't need to be a music expert to use it; the songs are easy to learn and fun to sing. Good quality resources are of paramount importance in teaching, and this is first rate."

—*GAP Good Autism Practice*

Music provides a unique and powerful means of promoting communication and social interaction in students with learning difficulties. In this collection, Pat Lloyd brings together 46 songs composed or adapted for use with children with communication problems.

Each of the songs features a vocal line and piano accompaniment and can be listened to on the audio CD included with the book. Simplified guitar versions are also provided for a selection of the songs. Pat Lloyd provides suggestions for how each song can be used and developed to encourage communication and social interaction, and lists a range of possible objectives for each one. Advocating a flexible approach, she demonstrates how musical activity can be adapted easily and successfully to the specific needs of individual students.

Enjoyable and easy to use, this is an ideal resource for specialist and non-specialist music instructors working to improve the communication and social skills of students with learning difficulties, including those with additional autism.

Pat Lloyd, M.Ed., is a qualified music therapist and teacher who has worked in the field of special needs for over 25 years, both in special schools and for the NHS. Her roles have ranged from music specialist teacher to Deputy Head. She currently works as an advanced skills teacher and music therapist at Heritage House School in Buckinghamshire, UK, and also as a regional tutor for the University of Birmingham on the Webautism program.